YO DON'T KNOW JACK

by Susan Pryor

YOU DON'T KNOW JACK
by Susan Pryor

ISBN: 978-1-935018-39-1

Copyright ©2010 Susan Pryor

All rights reserved by Susan Pryor
Please email the author at:
jpryor001@stny.rr.com
for permission to republish or reprint any portion
of this book.

PUBLISHED BY:
Five Stones Publishing
A DIVISION OF:
The International Localization Network
randy2905@gmail.com
ILNcenter.com

Table of Contents

INTRODUCTION 5
LET 'ER DRIP 7
FIRST DATE 11
THE WEARING O' THE GREEN 15
REVELATION 23
A BOLT FROM THE BLUE 25
MOON RIVER 29
MALAPROPISMS 37
SAILING, SAILING ...(OR, THE RACE FOR THIRD PLACE) 39
VIET NAM 45
THINK PINK 51
MORE MALAPRYORISMS 55
IMMERSED IN HIS WORK 57
SKI BUM 61
TILES in TIBERIAS 67
BOB 73
LET'S FACE IT 77
FILL 'ER UP!! 79
WILD ONE 83
OH, DEER! 85
THE TEETOTALER 89
HIS JUST DESSERTS 91
THE I'S HAVE IT 93
PRESERVING THE POINSETTIAS 95
JUST PUTTERING AROUND 101
GOLF---2008 105
FALLING OUT 109

INTRODUCTION

Has it ever happened to you?

All too often it has to me. I am referring to those occasions when I found myself at a funeral home visiting with a family who had lost a loved one and only then thinking of all the nice things I wish I had said to or about that person. And I speak of those sometimes awkward moments that arrived during funeral services when the minister asked if anyone wanted to share a remembrance of the departed and I was too shy, scared or reluctant to do so.

Often, after such a time, I indulged in self recrimination. Then one day, while again condemning myself for cowardice and lack of compassion, it struck me! If we all have so many pleasant, funny or thoughtful things to say about people when they are dead, why shouldn't we have the same things to say about them while they are alive?

Pondering this, I could readily see that spreading good news about the living while they were living could instantly affect lives in our families, churches, and neighborhoods. More immediately, it could have an impact in my own home.

I am married to a remarkable man named Jack. His kindness is legendary; his humor is a delight. People wait in lines for his hugs. Why should I wait to tell people that? Of more importance, why should I wait to tell Jack that?

An additional thought came. Rather than speak words that may or may not be heard or remembered, why not create a more permanent testimonial? Thus was born the idea for this book. Its pages are a short account of the thoughts, feelings, attitudes and ways that make Jack so unique. In some ways it is a mini biography. Necessarily omitting the early years before I knew him, it recounts a few but telling highlights of our last forty-six years together. In other ways it is a book of revelation as it describes the life events, changing personality, and developing character that continue to forge him into a man of integrity. Finally it is my tribute to a remarkable, loving, patient man who gave me the highest honor when he asked me to be his wife.

If you don't think these weeks and months at my desk were worth it, you don't know Jack.

LET 'ER DRIP

Some men and women have captivating stories about how they met their mates. A few, for example, tell about becoming acquainted with their husbands or wives while on a mercy mission or as members of a dangerous mountain trek. More poignantly, others remember encountering their spouses under dreadful circumstances such as huddling in close quarters in an air raid shelter during the bombing of London or surviving a plane crash. Even more have romantic beginnings, perhaps finding true love on a blind date. While adventure, intense feelings or romance do legitimately signal the beginning of many a marriage, for a few, happening on their life's love seems but a matter of chance.

Jack and I fall under this last category. Our meeting can best be labeled as just circumstance or serendipity. But was it? For us, what might have been perceived as an ordinary moment of every day life turned into an extraordinary moment that affected the rest of our lives.

So it was at Alfred University, the mother of men, in the fall of 1962. Jack was a senior that year and I but a lowly sophomore. He was well known, at least among the girls on campus, for his happy manner, joy of life---and bright red car. Suffice it to say that my life was blessed with none of these. Yet, somehow, someway, all that changed in a moment.

One lovely fall day a blood bank had been scheduled at the school. I was underweight and shouldn't even have been thinking about giving blood but since it was for such a priceless cause, I decided to do so anyway. When the nurse who signed people in found out I had low blood pressure as well as a few missing pounds she asked me not to give blood at all or, if I still insisted on doing so, to sign a disclaimer freeing her organization of any problems I might have after doing so. So determined was I to donate blood that I signed the document.

Only a few moments later I was ushered into a large room with a multitude of cots. There I was told to lie down and roll up my sleeve. A nurse came over to me, showed me all the equipment that would be used and explained the blood donation process. Then came the prick of a needle.

From seeing news articles and hearing friends' stories of donating blood, I thought that blood would quickly gush from my arm, flow down the plastic tube, fill the collection bag and I would be out of there in five minutes. Maybe it was the low blood pressure but flow it did not. I watched as one drop of blood slowly trickled down the tube and into the bag. A moment later another drop oozed out of my arm and began the slow journey to the collection point. This I could see was going to be a long afternoon.

Somewhere in the midst of this prolonged extraction there was a flurry of activity to my right. Another donor was being bedded down. Another cute donor was being given the scoop on blood donation. Another very cute donor was connected from arm to tube to bag. But, just as it was supposed to happen, this donor's blood was really flowing. Compared to mine, it was seemed to be gushing out as it quickly filled his bag.

Suddenly New Donor looked over at me. "Hi," he said. "I'm Jack." Since counting blood drops had become somewhat boring, I introduced myself to him as well and we began to talk. His bag was as full in five minutes as mine was after half an hour.

The nurse came back to check on things and saw my dilemma. To help me--or hurry me--she rolled a cloth into a ball and handed it to me telling me to squeeze it every few seconds to increase the rate of blood flow. Sure enough! Seeping turned into a more steady drip.

She then looked at Jack's now full bag, commended him highly, disconnected him from his tube, put a band aid on his puncture site, told him to wait a few moments, sit up slowly, wait a few more moments, and then go into another room for some juice and cookies before going back to classes.

It was disappointing to know I had but a few more moments to enjoy his company. Then I perked up considerably when I heard him say, "I'll wait for you out in the lounge. When you finish here, maybe we could go for a coke."

I didn't even have to decide whether or not to skip my next class.

Then he sat up.

Quickly.

Way too quickly.

Then he fainted and fell back on the cot.

Our nurse saw all this and was promptly there to

help. I just kept squeezing and squeezing. Jack just kept getting paler and paler. Then I thought, "You dummy! If you fill this bag up now, you'll have to leave and will never get a chance to talk to him again."

Too late. The pumping stopped. My bag was full. The nurse stabilizing Jack saw this and called in an aide who disconnected me and then went through the same basic instructions for recovery: wait a bit; sit up slowly; wait a bit more; go to the other area to replace fluids and eat cookies for energy.

I waited as long as I could. He was still in another world.

I held the band aid on my arm as long as I could. Was it irony or was the arm I had been trying to get blood out of the same arm I was now trying to keep blood in? Jack was still gone.

I sat up slowly. Not even a flutter from the other cot.

I waited a bit more. Still out.

Finally, when the malingering was obvious and the need of my cot for the next donor was apparent, I got up slowly and went for the goodies. I ate and drank them very slowly. Jack was still in bed.

With a happy sigh that this had been a special afternoon and a sad sigh that I probably would never see Jack again, I left the Campus Center.

Chance?

Not a chance!

FIRST DATE

Several weeks followed in which the incident at the blood drive drifted slowly into the past. While gone, it was not forgotten. Classes, term papers and exams kept time rolling by and dates and fun times with classmates and friends were enjoyed.

Like most other girls at college in the sixties, my home away from home was a dorm on campus. At Alfred University that year, my room was the second in a long line of rooms at one end of a seemingly endless corridor and the floor's only phone (yes, I know--who can believe the primitive condition of phone service in the Dark Ages?) was located at the far other end. To get our phone messages, on a rotating basis, a girl on the floor was assigned the job of answering the phone each night, finding out who was wanted, quietly walking to her room and informing her of her call. Occasionally, as we got to know each other better, she could act as the middle man, ask who was calling, and, if it was someone the girl being called didn't want to talk to, she would tell the caller the girl was out. More usually, after a few weeks of the same unwilling girl answering the phone all the time because her room was too close to it's constant shrill ringing, she would simply answer the phone and scream, "Hey, so and so. It's for you!"

One evening the phone in the dorm rang. Soon the dulcet tones of that night's phone answerer rang out, "Hey, Burkel, (my maiden name was Burke) come to the phone." Because of the combined roar of dozens of girls in a confined space who were typing, listening to radios and stereos, showering, using whirly sounding hair dryers and just plain talking, the first call for me to come to the phone was neither heard nor responded to. Sweet tones then turned into sirens of sound as the word again rang out, "BURKEL, ANSWER THE PHONE. IT'S SOME GUY!"

As I jogged down the hall I mentally reviewed any "guy" who might be calling. Father? Brother? Classmate? Arriving at the other end of the corridor I picked up the dangling receiver and heard, "Hi. This is Jack."

Some guy was right.

After fumbling my way through forgettable, foggy mumblings I finally understood that I was being asked on a date to a hobo party at his fraternity house. But, even sooner than that, did I want to meet him in a couple of days, go to a rummage sale that would be held in one of the churches in town, and find things for an appropriate costume? Then, after that, would I like to go for that long ago promised coke?

Did I?

And so we did. On the night of the party there we were. Suspenders, stretched to the breaking point, struggled to hold up baggy, pillow-stuffed pants. Cheeks and chins blackened by burnt cork created that ever popular scraggly-bearded look. Threadbare tweed jackets, oversized shoes that were difficult to keep on our feet, and grungy, floppy hats completed our ensembles.

In our mouths, cigar butts were clenched between our teeth for an added air of panache. Not a chance in a million of a romantic evening.

We arrived as the party was getting in full swing. There we met friends, laughed, and played around even as we admired other costumes of equal elegance. After a while, we and another couple decided to drive to a nearby small city where there was an Erie-Lackawanna train depot and a lot of railroad tracks in order to try out our hobo costumes on some professionals. Clever weren't we?

Somehow the train personnel were onto us. Not one train stopped. Not one whistle sounded. Not one real hobo joined us.

In no way discouraged, we determined to follow up this idea with an even better one. In full regalia, all four of us went to a nearby establishment called the Number One Club where a band was playing and the noise of merriment led us to believe that people were having a good time. At our entry though the music stopped. Two steps in the door and the good times were put on hold. Goggle eyed people stared as fake hobos invaded their space. It was only when it became clear that we meant no harm that the musicians again began playing.

While I would like to say that we began dancing, those enormous pillows and floppy shoes said no to anything that resembled back to back, belly to belly or cheek to cheek. When the regular patrons threw a total of twenty-three cents on the floor for our spending pleasure, we thought it might be time to go.

It was also edging closer to curfew, that magic hour when all girls living on campus had better be signed

13

into their dorms and back in their rooms or else. (Yes, life at college was a different world then.)

Opting for one more quick stop before that, we got back in the car and drove "down the road". That was a nightspot well known by AUers located between the city we were in and our school. There, meeting other fugitives from the hobo party, we again tried to dance. Arms around each other we, as best we could, slowly circled the room. It was then, in a moment as clear to me four and a half decades later as it was at that moment, that I heard a voice speak into my mind, "This is the man you are going to marry."

In spite of the noise of loud music, the uproar of revelry, and the constant clink and clank of bottles and glasses that created a din easily heard on the outside, I heard the voice from the inside repeat, "This is the man you are going to marry."

I couldn't have been more astonished. Wisdom dictated that I not share that news with Jack. I did look at him however. Really look at him. Instead of a funny hat I saw shiny dark hair. Rather than a blackened features now streaked with rivulets of sweat, I saw kind eyes and a handsome face. In place of the rest of his now shabby, falling apart costume I saw a patient, gentle, fun to be with, clean cut, wholesome young man, one I knew I could like.

What he saw as he looked back at me I do not know. I could only say to that Voice, "Fine with me. But You are the One who will have to tell him that."

THE WEARING O' THE GREEN

There comes a time in every growing relationship when the boy and girl who have met each other then have to meet each other's parents. At times this is an unspoken signal to those parents that their children's association is developing into something more than casual. Long before Jack or I thought we had any reason to make plans concerning such get-togethers, fate intervened. A few months after meeting at the blood drive and going on our first date, Jack had the distinction of meeting my parents. In fact, he met them quite literally by accident.

Because it was a good way to relax from classes, exams, papers, and studying and a fun way to get to know each other, life at Alfred University included spontaneous get-togethers and weekend parties. Additionally, there were four major college weekends built into the school calendar that were looked forward to every year: Fraternity and Sorority Weekends, Military Ball and St. Pat's Weekend. Since my parents were both the offspring of many generations of hardworking, enduring Irish, Jack's meeting them just before the St. Pat's celebration was appropriate. And surely memorable. As I recall......

All of us are aware of the frenzy and frolic that occur in the middle of March each year as people of Irish descent and those who wish they were gather to honor St. Patrick, the patron saint of Ireland. Among several other schools of study at AU, there is a ceramics college. Since, according to its tradition, St. Pat is the patron saint of ceramic engineers, honoring him on his special day took on an added local flavor and significance on campus. Truly, of the four special college festivities, to many St. Pat's Weekend was the premier event on the social calendar.

As can be well imagined, events such as this that involve a whole weekend and activate a whole campus don't just happen. In the School of Ceramics, the hub of all the excitement, preparations for such a huge undertaking began months before the actual weekend. Perhaps the most time consuming of these was making souvenirs--from ceramics, of course. Whether ash trays, small bowls, trivets, or special gifts to mark a particular St. Pat's celebration, the party favors were designed, molded, baked, rubber-scrubbed, glazed, fired in a kiln, and then cooled by ceramic students until row upon row of them were completed and stacked on every available storage space in the kiln room.

Even as these preparations were frantically apace in the clay and glass department the fraternities and sororities on campus began to plan their own events for the upcoming weekend, too. Each Greek house which chose to do so got involved by making a float. These usually began as tractors that pulled flat bed field equipment borrowed from local farmers. Not too festive in their normal state, they became regal works of art that Monet would have envied after they had been slowly but perfectly decorated from top to bottom with thousands of colorful flowers painstakingly crafted from tissue paper or kleenex. These were supposed to represent something near and dear to the fraternity or sorority sponsoring them. Occasionally some of them actually stuck to the St. Pat's theme, too.

As the date of the festivities grew closer, the fraternities had even more to do. No huge affair like this could pass without a gathering at their house. Many brothers, finally fed up with the softer side of life, pressed their girlfriends into the flower making detail so they could be free to plan how to entertain their guests at the upcoming party.

Finally the long awaited, yearly gala-to-end-all-galas arrived. Often accompanied by a snow storm and bone chilling winds, the weekend was a well coordinated series of events. Because it was their party, on Friday the celebration began with an open house at the Ceramics School. This was sometimes followed by a dress up dinner date.

On Saturday, it was parade time. Down the main street of Alfred, New York came a bevy of convertibles each bearing a lovely, shivering classmate who hoped to be chosen Queen of St. Pat's Weekend. These were followed by the famous floats which dazzled all as they passed by with every visible crack and crevice a riot of flowers and every grey plank on the field wagons embellished in beauty.

Later that evening after the campus parties came the grand finale--the St. Pat's Ball. In a decorated gym, a live band played for all those who had worked so hard

17

to create so much out of so little. Lovely evening gowns swirled past. Souvenirs were given away. The winners of the prizes for the best floats were announced and the Queen was crowned. For those of us privileged to enjoy the festivities, the memories weren't just for the weekend; they were for a lifetime.

There was another custom not yet spoken of that also began weeks before the St. Pat's Weekend of '63. That was the ritual growing of beards. In the deep, dark hall of tradition, someone had deemed it appropriate--even obligatory--that all men serving on the St. Pat's Counsel, the board overseeing the event, should celebrate the occasion by growing beards.

Grow them they did. Whether long or short, wispy or full, by late February or early March it was easy to spot Counsel members by their bushy cheeks and chins.

Jack was co-chair of St. Pat's Weekend that year and true to form, he grew a beard. This was not just a wimpy Van Dyke style beard straggling down his chin. Nor was it just sideburns hiding somewhere near his ears. This was a full face beard, immediately attractive for its abundance. As time went by a couple of other things drew attention to it as well. First, instead of just growing in a solid dark brown color like the hair on his head, this beard had a mind of its own. It capriciously decided that most of it would indeed be dark brown but the rest would be orange. Second, as the weekend neared and he got more into the party spirit, Jack added to this already bewildering kaleidoscope of color by dying his beard. When you looked at him, his forehead, eye area, and nose seemed normal in color; the rest of his face was a bright emerald green.

With this image of Jack in mind, let me now describe my parents. Irish, as stated. Perhaps severely so. Life had been hard-scrabble difficult for both father and mother when they were children and had not improved much in their adult years. Stoicism and military precision left over from serving in World War II marked my father's personality and rejection and pain my mother's. Green beards just for the fun of it did not enter into their world at all.

Then came the night. Then came the memorable occasion that acted as catalyst to bring such opposite people, Jack and my parents, together.

Perhaps a week or two before St. Pat's, Jack and I went out on a date. With another couple we enjoyed a movie in a nearby town. Coming out of the theater we noticed that it had been snowing. In fact, it had snowed a lot. To add to the wintry picture, it was cold and icy.

Since, after stopping for some refreshments, the weather showed no signs of improving we decided that our best plan was to go back to school while it was still safe to do so. Accordingly, we got in the car and began the twelve mile trek. Little did we know what was ahead.

At a place called the Beacon (earlier referred to as "down the road"), a car that was also on its way back to school had pulled out of the parking lot and then stalled when its battery failed. It came to a stop perpendicularly across the north-south lanes, dead in the road. Now knowing this, we and the couple with us were making our snowy way north. There was no warning. We rounded a curve in the road. The other car whose headlights were out of commission because of the battery situation was suddenly there in front of us. A collision was inevitable.

Jack did his best to save us by cranking his steering wheel hard to the right. Even while sliding on ice, we discovered that recently plowed snow now formed such a large crusty barrier along the side of the road that our car couldn't fit between the stalled car and the guard rail. After smashing into the other car we then, as I learned later, ended up atop the snow mound teetering on the guardrail.

Jack, at the same time, did his best to save me. In this pre-seatbelt era, when we crashed into the other car, inertia sent me flying forward. Seeing this, Jack, while steering with his left hand, reached out to me with his right. His intention was to get his hand in front of me to hold me back. Instead, he smacked me in the side of the head, pushed me into the window of the passenger's side door and knocked me out cold.

I am told that I was hauled out of the car by people at the scene, carried into the Beacon and laid out on a table. From there I was transported to a hospital in the town we had just come from. When I awoke and was having double vision the doctor in the emergency room decided to keep me in the hospital for observation for at least overnight.

The university had been busy, too. Immediately after hearing of the accident they called my parents who arrived the next afternoon. I can still read their faces: What happened ? Are you all right ? Who tried to kill our baby girl?

Into this chaos of a young adult trying to explain that all was well in spite of how things might look to older adults, of stoic Irish parents trying not to crack and show their feelings, of soldier-dad trying to organize this with military precision, of overwrought mom still imagining the worst instead of the best, the door of the hospital room opened. With relief I saw who is was. As he walked toward us I said, "Mom and Dad, I would like you to meet my friend, Jack."

Before I could explain to them that he had acted heroically in swerving so that none of the six or so college boys who were trying to push the stalled car out of the road were smashed into by his skidding car or that he had saved me from hitting if not going through the windshield, they both turned toward him. Already in conflict within themselves about meeting the driver of the car that crashed with their daughter in it, they took one look at Jack's bright green beard and froze.

My shocked mother turned to my amazed father. Grabbing his arm as if she needed him to hold her up, with all the pathos and emotion that can be wrung out of two terse words she simply said, "Oh, Ed."

That went well.

REVELATION

Soon I was declared well enough to be released from the hospital and return to school. With bandages covering my knees that had been lacerated when they hit the dashboard of the car and sporting a large lump on my head, I was all too eager to go.

Jack picked me up in a borrowed car and we returned to campus. Even as we passed the scene of the accident we talked about what had happened and how thankful we were that no one had been seriously injured.

When we reached my dorm, Jack walked me to the door and then, unexpectedly, came into the lounge. Seating us in a quiet corner, he said, "I haven't had much time to think about this but I've learned one thing. I didn't start dating you with any intention of getting serious. This accident has made me realize that my feelings have changed. I discovered that I didn't want to lose you.

My prayer was being answered. The Voice was speaking to him now, too.

A BOLT FROM THE BLUE

What he said was true. When Jack and I started seeing each other, neither of us had any intention of entering a serious relationship. After the fun of the hobo party though we began to date. At first, it was both sporadically since we were busy and casually since neither of us really wanted to get involved. As we saw more of each other that gradually changed. By Christmas, sporadically had become regularly and casually had become intentionally. Mid semester break seemed unusually long that year and when it was time to return to AU, I realized that for the first time I really wanted to get back to school. For more French classes and history lessons? I don't think so.

Jack and I met again soon after we both got back to campus and it was as if the three week interlude had never happened. January, February and the March madness of St. Pat's passed quickly. During that time I learned what it was to be invited to and enjoy those fraternity weekends compete with parties and dress-up balls. Possibly even more delightfully, I enjoyed walks in the snow and finding out that Wile E. Coyote was never going to catch the road runner, at least not at twenty-five cent movie night on campus.

Finally as it always does, spring broke through. It was then permissible to take off the first three layers of clothing needed to survive a wild and wooly western New York winter. Dress up dances turned into an occasional dinner date and long walks became even longer car rides.

One memorable April day, Jack and I were driving on the top of one of the many, tall, pine covered hills that surround the village of Alfred. We were looking for Foster's Lake to check out the lodge that was there for an upcoming social event. We were also lost.

No doubt to impress me that he was not like other men who would not ask for directions or look at a map when he didn't know where he was, Jack pulled off the road onto a cleared area that was similar to a utility company's right of way. He stopped the car directly under a a very tall TV cable antenna tower.

Even as he was doing so, it was very apparent that though there were still a lot of unmelted snow piles at this high altitude, spring was on its way. Grass was greening, yellow wild flowers festooned stubby fields and water that had recently been held captive in ice formations was trickling past us and flowing its merry way down the hill.

If spring was on its way, so was a storm. Not a snow storm on this fine spring day, but a spine chilling extravaganza complete with ear shattering thunder and lighting flashes that would make any Fourth of July fireworks display pale in comparison.

However, we missed all that. In our cosy car parked under the metal tower looking at maps had turned into other things. We called it necking. It didn't involve sex, drugs, or booze but with the right person, it was delightful.

With all sense of time and space removed, neck we did as the storm drew closer. With all input from human senses on hold, neck we did as thunder growled and lightning slashed its cryptic messages across the heavens. We were still enjoying each others company when the sky darkened to almost black and rain that might have made the deluge of Noah's Ark fame seem like a trickle of water in comparison came roaring down.

It was sometime later in this state of stormy wonder that I heard a strange noise. It wasn't the crash of thunder that caught my attention but an odd pop-crackly sound. Simultaneously I smelled the unmistakable odor of sulphur. To add to the alarms that my reawakened senses of sound and smell were issuing, I saw an awesome sight. The whole car was outlined in shimmering electric blue and the radio antenna was frantically whipping back and forth.

Jack was able to come back to reality in a flash. His accurate reaction to all this unusual frenzy was, "My God, we've been hit by lightning."

I didn't leave the utopia on the hilltop and return to the real world as quickly. My befuddled reaction was, "Boy, can this guy kiss!"

Even as we both came to realize that the car, or something in the very close vicinity had indeed been struck by lightning and that we were blessed to be alive the storm began to ease off. Torrents of rain became but a steady downpour and then stopped altogether. The once inky sky lightened to a normal spring afternoon glow. Gradually the thunder rolled away to the next hill and the lightning skipped ahead of it to see what new mischief it could cause elsewhere.

We looked at each other with an after the fact knowledge of the danger we had been in and yet all seemed well. When we felt it was safe to do so we got out of the car to look around. Except for four tires that had melted into flat, gooey pancakes where the tread met the ground there were no signs of trauma. Forgetting our search for Foster's Lake, we reentered the car and roll-plopped, roll-plopped our way back to school on the weirdly shaped tires. As he walked with me to the dorm and we said goodbye, all we could do it look at each other in wonder.

As days passed and I had time to ponder that electric afternoon several things stood out to me:

Men and women react to dramatic situations in entirely different ways. In today's world that would mean that men are indeed from Mars and women from Venus.

My high school physics teacher really meant it when he said that metal (the tower), water (the rain), and electricity (the lightning) don't mix.

The aftermath of our adventure with the lightning bolt told me things about the state of my heart. The young man I liked after the hobo party and knew I could honor and respect was now a young man I cared for deeply. Now it was I who would have been devastated had I lost him. Liking him was turning to loving him.

MOON RIVER

As it turned out, the Voice had accurately announced our future. That fall, Jack went to graduate school. After a two year course at Wharton School of Business at the University of Pennsylvania in Philadelphia, he would earn his MBA in business management. While this was a wonderful preparation for life, there was a problem. Philadelphia was a long way from Alfred where I was still going to school. In fact, it was a six hour trip to drive between the two. The separation proved much more difficult than anticipated. His coming north for an occasional weekend was a big investment in time and money and a big let down emotionally when he left. After a while the question kept arising: why couldn't I complete the studies for my degree in Philadelphia?

A year and a month after our first date, Jack proposed to me. With justified hesitation and concern in four sets of parents' eyes, one month later, without the green beard, we were married. Between semesters, in a church decorated with poinsettias, garland, and the beauty of Christmas, amid family and friends we said the familiar vows. After a brief honey moon, I found myself moving south. Having transferred to a new college, I too was now a resident of Philadelphia.

Many things stand out about those first few months of marriage. Among them:

I didn't know how to cook--or bake--or even boil. Poor Jack!

For two waifs from the hills and dales of rural western New York, life in a city was a whole new world. Like the day I stepped over a man lying in a gutter who I thought was drunk. In truth according to the evening news, he was dead. Or like the day our car with so many AU memories was stolen.

As with most college students, finances were a problem. Down time therefore had to be cheap time. Each week after long days of commuting, labs, homework and doing all the extras that are required to pass certain classes, Friday nights were a highly anticipated respite. As soon as we both got home, the festivities began. First on the madcap program, we splurged on dinner. Chicken pot pies were three for a dollar in those days so instead of just eating one each, we made a meal of all three. After that indulgence, we pulled out the hide-a-bed that occupied way too much space in the tiny living room of our apartment and made a huge bowl of popcorn. Movies on TV, though usually involving giant, angry ants or green ooze that ate people, were free. Our goal was to see who could stay awake the longest, eat the most popcorn, and make up the best ending for the movie because the person who fell asleep first would never know the difference anyway. In reality, we both fell asleep mid movie and awoke the next morning swimming in a sea of popcorn, salt, butter, and corn kernels with neither of us remembering how it all turned out.

In the spring of '65, there was a chance for a rare and different weekend celebration. At a night club in New Jersey, Andy Williams was to be in concert. This was THE Andy Williams who could melt anyone's butter with his warm, mellow voice. This was THE Andy Williams who sang the lovely, haunting song, Moon River. Eerily, our lives reflected the words of the tune. We felt like two drifters (away from home) off to see the world (Philadelphia). And in Philadelphia there was such a lot of world to see. There were malls bigger than the whole downtown section of the village I grew up in, parks, gardens, a zoo, museums and a uniquely impressive array of historical sites where the bravery and determination of the men who had sired and the women who had birthed this nation still spoke volumes. To honor Mr. William's plea to see it all, we decided to stretch our boundaries by going to see him.

So save we did. Any way we could gain even a penny was tried. We cut back to one pot pie, gave up lunches, and even did less laundry at the laundromat.

Finally the big night came. We left our apartment, drove to New Jersey, found the night club and, in our best man and woman of the world smiles, opened the door and approached the usher. It was then that we discovered that if we really wanted to be admitted to that concert, we should have made reservations months before the event. There were, we were informed, no tickets left for us.

Again shocked at how things worked in a city compared to the ease of life in the country where there weren't usually enough people to make up a crowd so there was no need to worry about the number of seats, we turned to go.

It might have been Jack's crestfallen look or the tears streaming down my face but suddenly, the usher had a change of heart. Miraculously, seating for two more was available. Literally the last two people to be admitted, into the club we went.

As Jack went to hang up our coats, I followed our guide to our table. There I found myself staring at fourteen other perfectly dressed and coifed older ladies, all good friends and all annoyed at the late intrusion. Our- -to be charitable in my description--hard boiled, surly waitress came over to our table and set out sixteen glasses of water. Even as she left, Jack belatedly arrived and hurriedly found his place beside me at one end of the long table. Unfortunately, in seating himself, his knee hit the table leg with such force that he knocked over every one of the water glasses.

Such tut-tutting. Such tsking. There was a flurry of activity as everyone present grabbed tissues and napkins and tried to sop up the water that was cascading toward them. Though unhappy that they would have to sit through the upcoming performance with wet laps and damp chairs, they accepted Jack's apology with profound grace and once again settled down for the concert.

As soon as our soggy situation didn't require her to do anything for us, our waitress came back. Without preamble she announced that we were allowed two drinks, that we had to order them immediately, that she would bring them both at the same time for our drinking pleasure and that once the show started she would not be back to wait on us again.

I now found out that I was seated among pros who had enjoyed many such nightclub events. Faster than Mohammed Ali could throw a punch, each of the ladies ordered just what she wanted. Since my expertise at ordering drinks was somewhat limited I wavered between lemonade and some concoction with the name Tom in it. Exasperated at the delay, Miss Congeniality finally spit out that she would bring me the same drinks that some of the others were having. Disappearing for about a minute, she reappeared with a huge tray on which thirty-two drinks were perfectly balanced. She slammed it down in front of us, distributed the drinks, and then thankfully left us in peace.

As the lights went down, the announcer came on stage to tell us that before Andy Williams began his concert we would be entertained by a singing family whose star was rising in the show biz world. We were among the privileged to meet its youngest member, Donnie. With that he introduced the Osmond Family who bounced onto stage and launched into song. So excited was he to see and hear them that Jack quickly turned to his left to get a better view. Too quickly as it turned out. Again knee and table leg collided. Again, unbelievably, amazingly, incredibly, the table tipped. And again, the immediate result was a plethora of very full glasses tipping and spilling their contents all over the party goers nearest them. First two fell. Then the next two tipped and the next two, each pair in perfect, synchronized slow motion, until all were lying empty as they adorned the inundated table top in gaudy disarray. Moon River was no competition for this raging river of liquorish brew that was spreading everywhere.

What a mess. Cherries were fighting with pineapple bits. Little umbrellas weren't keeping anyone dry. Tiny swords stabbed everyone in sight. Red wine, white wine, rum, gin, whiskey, and a few other unknown liquids joined forces to form a sticky, gooey tidal wave of colors and flavors that rolled off the table, dripped down onto our laps, and then dribbled to the floor.

There was no little commotion as we all jumped to our feet and tried to avoid the oncoming flood. We whipped out the soggy handkerchiefs we had used to pat ourselves down after the first watery bath to now mop up the spill and dry ourselves from the second. True to her word, our waitress did not return. She didn't show up with napkins, brooms, or mops, or even to offer her condolences. Then we sat in soaked silence while Andy Williams finished his concert.

When it was over fourteen ladies rose as one and, while attempting to shield their drenched, fruit covered clothing from the stares of other patrons, cleared the area in about one minute flat. No lingering over goodbyes there. Two of us, not wanting to be seen by them again, waited for an extra moment before fleeing the scene of the crime. Then we began giggling. Then laughing.

Into this scene of hilarious devastation came Little Miss Sunshine. As Jack left to find our coats, she who had given us drinks of her preference and timing rather than ours, she who had been suspiciously absent when the first liquid river flowed and conspicuously missing for the second was now present and holding out her hand toward me.

Was she asking for help? Was she seeking forgiveness for such dereliction of duty and unspeakably cranky, rude service? No! The intimidating, in-my-face, repeated rubbing of her first three fingers against her thumb was the universal sign that she wanted money. Unbelievably, she was seeking a tip!

Sadly or not, just as we rustics had not known to make reservations, so also we didn't know about tipping. Sadly or not, overstretched financially as we were to even attend the concert, we had no money to give her anyway. Besides, in my few months in Philadelphia, I had learned a bit about manipulation. I therefore made it clear to her that even if I could offer her money, after what we had just been through no amount of belated, strong armed tactics would induce me to give her any.

Not taking that as a no, the moment Jack returned with our coats, she confronted him and even more urgently, even more adamantly repeated her gesture.

Poor woman! She truly didn't know with whom she was dealing. Every gene in Jack's DNA oozed optimism. He wasn't called Jolly Jack for nothing. Because he ignored the seamy side of life, he rarely even recognized it. Conversely, because he courted the sunny side of life, his behavior reflected it. He was not then and is not to this day a keen judge of intimidating, coercive behavior.

When our waitress shook her outstretched hand at him he really didn't know what she wanted. He hesitated a moment as he tried to process her message. Then the lights came on. Without even a glimmer that her gesture was a demand for money, when she reached out to him yet again, he reached out to her too. He took her hand in his, shook it warmly and, as only he could do, sincerely thanked her for a pleasant evening.

She was still stunned when he gathered me up and we left with our Moon River memories. In my last over-the-shoulder glimpse, her hand may have been empty but there was a smile on her face.

MALAPROPISMS

The dictionary defines a malapropism as the incorrect or in appropriate use of a word. While in college though Jack may have earned degrees in Ceramic Engineering and Business Administration, he seemed to have missed the English department. So adept has he become in the art of verbal blunders that we, his family and friends, now refer to some of his more memorable linguistic goofs as malapryorisms.

For instance, I'll bet you never knew that the literary classic, The Lady of the Lake, was written by Sir Walter Squat.

Regarding weather, one wet fall day he said he had heard that the next few days were going to be cloudy with a trace of participation. Shortly after that he told me that we were due for our first serious snow flaw.

Jack also has a thing about food. In his argot pretzels are prenzils. Smores are made of graham crackers, chocolate bars and mushrooms. The stuff that hangs down from southern oak trees is Spanish Rice. And the head of a marching band is the drum margarine. Recently, while at a family birthday dinner, he enjoyed every delicious bite of his lack of ram.

Although he has the directional instincts of a homing pigeon, he is sometimes unable to describe things well.

As he tells is, one day he went to the Y to pump leather. After we once went to a museum to view the work of a world famous sculptor he referred to it as going to the Rodent Exhibit. When I asked him why he was so late one evening he said that on the way home he had gotten mislaid. That must be because Bethleham in right next to Jeruslaham.

Apparently it didn't occur to him that he was confusing a recent trip to Virginia Beach with the seamier side of life when he vented his outrage at people who think they won't get caught in their anti-social activities when they plant their cabanas in pots in their basements or hide them out in their fields.

SAILING, SAILING....
(OR, THE RACE FOR THIRD PLACE)

Long years ago when Jack was a teenager his parents bought a summer cottage on a small lake near their home. Too far west and too small to be considered one of New York State's famous Finger Lakes, it nevertheless was a place of beauty, peace, and fun. Sharing its name with another lake in the Adirondack Mountains, this lovely Eden in Western New York, boasting a unique flavor all its own, was called Loon Lake.

Since this lake and cottage were close enough for his father to commute to work, Jack and his family could stay at the lake and enjoy the long, lazy days of summer. Jack in particular reveled in this arrangement. He spent hours, days, weeks and months chasing turtles, swimming, ramming around in his beaten up old boat, water skiing, or just doing nothing in the sun. As he grew older another activity claimed more and more of his attention. When he learned to sail, other pastimes began to pale in comparison.

His first sailing adventures were on small boats called Sailfish. Essentially these were flat, wooden boards with a mast and a sail. Any who sailed on them were not in the comfort zone. With no place to put body parts, their straight surfaces meant that all aboard had to sit with feet and legs bent, turned or squished into awkward positions. Further, with the intent of keeping all sailors on the board, (or at least delay their departure into the lake) they also featured a sand-papery covering over the seating area on the wide board.

These mighty craft were known for two things: first was their innate ability to tip over for no reason at all at any time at all, and second their innate ability to wear the seat out of any bathing suit in just one afternoon of sliding over the rough, raspy board.

When the Sailfish was mastered, Jack progressed on to the Sunfish. Though about the same size, this sailboat was a huge jump in engineering. Besides its mast and sail, this beauty had a fiberglass shell complete with a well for storing legs and a strap for tucking feet and toes under. Since Jack's derriere could now be parked on the edge of the boat and his feet beneath him for both balance and security there was no need for a sandpapered seat. Oh, the joy of the sun and the sail on long lovely breezy afternoons.

Then things got really heady. As small as Loon Lake was, it was large enough to have a fleet. Several other families had learned the joys of sailing and one by one they bought a class of boats called Snipes. When twenty of so of these graced the sparkling lake waters, a boat club was officially sanctioned and an era like no other at Loon Lake began.

The races were on. Every Sunday afternoon from Memorial Day to Labor Day buoys were laid out and boats were rigged with sails, centerboards, and rudder. When ready they approached the starting line, jockeyed for a good position, and then, after a deafening blast from the starting gun which echoed up and down the lake, they were off. Sails unfurled, limbs straining, boats surging, each sailing team, captain and his crew, vied to be the first around the prearranged course and over the finish line.

One such Sunday, Jack and his dad were sailing in their bright red snipe named Topsy. It was a beautiful day and all was going well for them. A promising breeze was blowing and they were so adept at securing their feet under the straps in the well of the boat, sitting as far out on the edge of the boat as they could, leaning back so that their torsos, shoulders, and heads were even farther out of the boat (known as hiking out) and letting the ropes out so that the sails could catch the most wind that they were actually leading the race.

However, as many a sailor has learned over the years, the winds on Loon Lake are capricious. The promising breeze became playful. It blew strongly in some areas of the lake and died down in others. Sometimes its light puffs were followed by windy gusts and at other times zephyrs daintily ruffed the sails just before heavy gales tore at them. All in all it was a great day to have fun but pay attention.

Soon the tension began to mount. Observing that hiking out was giving the Pryor boat a decided advantage, a couple of other valiant sailors began to try this too. Little by little they were slowly gaining on Jack and his father.

On this particular day the finish line of the race was located directly in front of a point of well forested land. The old and gracious trees not only snuggled several gorgeous summer homes but they also shielded them from the onslaughts of the wind.

As Jack and his dad rounded the final buoy and began the last leg of the race toward the finish line they noticed that two other boats were now close behind them. Having led for so long there was no way they were going to let anyone pass them. Still in open water they thought that a final burst of speed might bring them in as winners. Seeing a breeze coming they adjusted ropes and sails and again hiked out as far as they could. So ready were they that as soon as the gust hit, they took off. They skimmed. They planed. They flew across the lake.

But suddenly, instead of being in open water they were sailing in front of the point of land. The wind gust that had been pushing them ever closer to glory was now blocked by land and trees. It died. Instantly their sailboat, with no wind in its sails and unbalanced because Jack and his father were still hiking out for all they were worth, lived up to its name.

Topsy turvied.

When the wind died Topsy simply took the path of least resistance. She bowed to the four hundred plus pounds of weight pulling her to the right and, before anyone could move or change a thing, she capsized. Turning completely over, she dumped two astonished sailors into the lake. Center board intact but upended and reaching for the sky, she looked like a red shark, floating around her victims.

Some onlookers later commented that the Pryors might have had a previous history of sail boat incidents because they reacted so well. Those earlier experiences did not fail them. Even as they sputtered, treaded water, and checked to see that the other was all right, they found themselves still clutching the ropes from the sails. As they did so they learned a secret. The slow, steady pulling on the lifelines told them that the boat was still moving. Mr. Newton was proven right yet again. Moving objects do indeed keep moving unless acted upon by an outside force--even in the water. Not only was Topsy still moving, but, incredibly, her momentum was propelling her toward the finish line.

Just then one boat passed them.

Then a second boat did too.

By unspoken agreement, Jack and his dad determined not to concede defeat. If Topsy wasn't done racing, neither were they. They didn't want to be the only sailors in the history of snipe racing whose boat finished the race with no one aboard. Neither did they want to be the only sailors in the history of snipe racing who had to swim past the finish line. Yes, veterans of incidents that ended up when dry people had gotten wet, they knew exactly what to do.

As Topsy surged on, they pulled themselves hand over hand along the ropes and slowly drew close to her. Then they were beside her. With just a little difficulty they clambered up on her. Using the center board as a lever, they again used their weight to force her up and out of the water. Ever so slowly Topsy responded. As if embarrassed that her top parts were now down and her bottom parts were exposed and up, she agreed to make things right.

Yielding to the pressure exerted on her by two impatient sailors, she half righted herself. After resting for just a moment on her side in the water, three things happened almost simultaneously.

First, Topsy decided to stop being so contrary. With a great splash, she fully righted herself.

Next, amazingly, Jack and his dad did not again fall off the wildly bucking boat. Countering her every move with weight shifts, when she came upright they just popped right back into her like two happy monkeys.

Finally, as the roar of laughter rose from the watches on shore, they crossed the finish line. Yes, indeed, riding low and sitting in a pool of water, they were the third place finishers.

Later, as the winners of the race were officially announced, Jack noticed Topsy's final salute to them. The Greeks may have had their wreaths to crown their victors but Topsy had a better plan. After the shouting died down, no two men ever more proudly sailed for home than did Jack and His dad with their third place cup and their laurel wreath, a giant gob of seaweed, still crowning the top of their mast.

Unfazed by all this, in later years when Topsy had been retired, Jack was crew on another sailboat from Look Lake that won the New York State Junior Snipe Championships.

Without the seaweed.

VIET NAM

While determination may have won Jack a trophy in sail boat racing it was courage that brought him to and through a long year in Viet Nam.

During his years at Alfred University he had joined the Reserve Officer Training Corp or ROTC. When he graduated in the early '60s he and those classmates who had completed this military program were commissioned as second lieutenants. Already the drum beat of war was in the air. Deferred from active duty for two years, when he graduated from Wharton in May, 1965, the winds of war were blowing strongly.

Knowing he would be called up at anytime we said goodbye to our two happy years in Philadelphia. After accepting an interim job at a manufacturing plant in Corning, New York, we settled there to learn about life after college. In May, 1966, the summons came. Uncle Sam was calling. He would be pleased if Jack would report to active duty at an army base in Maryland.

As an alarming number of soldiers were being sent to South East Asia it was said that an only son of an only son was exempt from military duty in an active war zone. Rumor or not, this only son of an only son who himself had no son had a different view. Perhaps a necessary reality for some or a perfect out for others, he wanted no part of not going where his country was asking him to go. As he said, "Someone will look out for me."

In Maryland where we sweltered in sizzling heat and sweated in oppressive humidity (just out of school and on army pay, an air conditioner was NOT an option) he was assigned to the army's Maintenance and Supply branch. In training programs there, in Virginia and finally in Texas he continued to grow and learn even as the day of deployment drew near. We still laugh that his jungle training took place in the deserts of western Texas. Way to go, army.

In June of 1967, the day arrived. The day we had been dreading was upon us. Classroom training was over. It was time to go to war.

His parents came, we said our goodbyes and three of us left for home driving across country from Texas to New York State. Jack and his unit left for Oakland, got aboard a ship and spent most of a month on the high seas heading for Asia. Never once, as reported by his astonished and envious shipmates, did he have the grace to join them in doing what comes naturally over the rails of a pitching, lurching ship. Surely it was all of that earlier sailing at Look Lake that helped his stomach survive.

Immediately upon arriving in Viet Nam Jack was sent to the Mekong Delta to a town named Can Tho where there was a large maintenance and supply depot. Describing his duties generally, he was one of many junior officers who were assigned to keep the army ready for any battle or campaign; they were to be well prepared for any situation, keep things going during any situation and to pick up the pieces after any situation, mend them, and get things ready for the next event.

More specifically, because of his business and military training, Jack was given a special designation. Branded with a title that only the military could think up or understand he became an MRE or a Material Readiness Expeditor. That meant that with a paper signed by General Westmoreland himself Jack could requisition any supplies or any men at any time to perform his duties. Imagine his delight the few times he had to bump generals and their staffs off helicopters or jeeps so he could use them to get much needed mechanics or supplies where they were desperately needed.

Sometimes his duty as an MRE led to fun times. More accurately, it led to short respites from the grind of dirt, sweat, heat and war. Part of his job in the Delta was to oversee the repair of boats used to carry supplies up and down the Mekong River. Of course, after they were overhauled they had to be tested to make sure they were fully serviceable again. Perhaps those long summers at the lake came into play here, too. Checking the boats by running them on the river with one driver aboard led to doing so with a whole crew of off duty soldiers. Taking this pleasure one step further, one day one of those resourceful young men came to the river with two crudely sawn boards and a long rope. From that day on After Maintenance Boat Testing featured an American soldier water skiing behind the boat as it flew across the water.

At Loon Lake, according to law all water skiing was done with one driver, a skier and a spotter. While the driver looked forward the spotter looked back at the skier to make sure all was well and to relay instructions, made by hand signal, from skier to driver. Skiing in Nam was similar but with a twist. Yes, there was a driver. Yes, there were skiers and a spotter. But, on the Mekong River, the spotter had an additional duty. While he did watch and he did relay information he also carried a loaded rifle so he could shoot any sharks which thought that skiers who fell into the water might be good for lunch.

While his job as an MRE sometimes resulted in fun times, it more often than not, led to dangerous ones. Much of the fighting in Viet Nam took place in open field. Much also occurred in four sided fire forts located out in the jungle. These were fortified areas roughly in the shape of a square that housed one hundred fifty-five millimeter field artillery pieces carefully placed to protect each side. If one of those guns broke down that side of the fort was totally vulnerable to attack or infiltration by a determined enemy. If this was a dangerous situation in daytime it was especially so at night.

When a gun jammed or failed, the person in charge of the fort made a hurry-up call to the nearest maintenance people. If the call came to Can Tho and it was Jack's turn to respond, he requisitioned a helicopter, flew to the area and checked the gun to see what was wrong and what was required to fix it. He then flew to the nearest storage depot, found the parts and the mechanics who could work wonders with those guns, flew back with them to the fort, got the gun back on line and choppered home. If the gun couldn't get fixed in daylight hours he and his crew remained at the fort and became part of the fighting force that repelled the attack everyone knew was coming on the vulnerable side of the fort that night. The threat of enduring that was really good incentive to get the repairs done quickly.

One day, Jack went to a site, flew out to get his needed men and material, flew back and oversaw the repairs. Since it was still daylight he and his pilot opted to fly back to their base at Can Tho. As they were lifting off some enemy forces who had infiltrated too close to the fort opened fire. There were tense moments as the ping of bullets on metal was heard. Their helicopter made some strange noises, momentarily gyrated out of control and wildly thrashed around. Just as suddenly it calmed down so Jack and his pilot continued on, arriving back at their base without any further problems.

When they landed, they found a mechanic and told him they had been in that helicopter when it had been fired on. To err on the side of caution they asked him to check the aircraft before anyone else flew in it.

Soon he came back to them.

"How did this helicopter get here," he asked?

Again they explained that they had flown it there after being fired on out near the fire fort.

Digesting that, the mechanic tried again. "When did you fly it here," he now asked?

Getting curious at the mechanic's odd questions the pilot responded, "This afternoon. We came under fire and heard some shots hit it but it was too dangerous to land and check things out so we flew it from there to here today."

Growing more perplexed with every answer, the mechanic then asked, "How long was the flight?"

When the pilot said it had taken about twenty minutes he got very quiet. "No," he said, "that is not possible. You couldn't have flown this chopper anywhere. The main rotor is all shot up. There is no way it could have stayed in the air."

The only son of the only son did indeed have Someone looking out for him.

THINK PINK

Jack may not have had a son when he left for Viet Nam but, a year later he had a daughter when he came home.

Back in the '60s there was no such thing as an instant pregnancy test. Women who hoped or questioned whether they were en route to parenthood had to wait six long weeks before their bodies or their doctors told them the news. Imagine our joy then that less than a week before he deployed we had a tender moment when I could share my news with Jack: he was going to be a father.

After he left I went home to enjoy what was expected to be a normal pregnancy and birth. My calendar revolved around two dates: our child's birth in January and Jack's return in June.

Somewhere in those months though, things went badly awry. We had planned to have our child born in his hometown. One weekend however, knowing that my time for traveling would soon be over I went to visit my parents who still lived in the town where I had been born. There the unexpected happened.

Without warning I found myself in the emergency room of the local hospital. From there I was quickly shuttled to the maternity department. Twenty minutes after my arrival, our daughter was born. Apparently all those days of pain arcing across and then settling in my lower back were labor pains. I was now a mother.

A family friend who was the regional Red Cross representative heard about all this. Personally and persistently, making phone call after phone call, she steadily worked her way up the military chain of command. Steadfastly refusing to be denied, her efforts were finally rewarded when she reached Jack on a field phone unit in the Mekong Delta and announced the news. Cigars and tears were the order of the day.

While Mrs. Rose had managed to reach Jack and tell him of his baby's birth she did not know and therefore had not told him all the details. It was not January when his daughter was born but November which made her a full two months premature. In the delivery room it was obvious that there were birth defects. Overnight in the nursery she developed jaundice. Soon it was apparent that there were neurological issues, too.

I was devastated. How could this have happened? Where was the dream of the all-American family? How was I to deal with this? Essentially alone in an unfamiliar environment and having to trust capable but unknown doctors life had to go on. And what if anything should I say to Jack?

During that time counselors advising family or friends about communicating with military personnel in a war zone warned against sending bad news. They especially frowned on the infamous Dear John letters sent by not-so-faithful ones who wanted to break off relationships. These (the army feared) might compromise the emotional stability and therefore the performance of troops in combat situations.

Such counselors served a valid purpose and I respected their opinion but this was different. Slowly realizing that this was not a temporary situation but a life changing one for all of us, I evaluated things and came to two conclusions: this was news that I should share with Jack before someone else did and news he had to be aware of so he wouldn't be shocked when he returned home.

Thankful that the decision to tell or not to tell him the unsettling news was mine alone to make, I ignored the counselors' warnings and wrote a Dear Jack letter. It did not ask him out of a difficult situation; it asked him to share this very unplanned, different and difficult journey with me and his child.

In this earlier age, as there were no instant pregnancy tests so also there was no instant communication. Speaking by cellphone or beaming photos half way around the world were not options. Email and chat rooms did not exist. When I wrote to Jack I knew that even by airmail it might take weeks for my letter to reach him and more weeks for his reply to reach me. As I waited, I settled in to the daily challenge of survival.

As the days passed, I grew increasingly weary and concerned. Enforced twenty-four hour care giving took a heavy toll on my mental and physical reserves. I was anxious that our baby couldn't eat properly. I was scared when each subsequent visit to a doctor seemed to reveal more problems. I felt rejected and alone. I was glad then sad, angry and then afraid. Overriding all this mental and emotional turmoil was the growing concern about Jack's reaction to the problems presented by his daughter's birth.

I had been told that statistics. Seventy-five to eighty percent of men faced with similar situations abandoned home and family. What would he say? Would he even want to return? Could we think pink and get through this together or would this, coupled with the pressures of war, cause him to leave?

How ashamed of my fears I was when one day his answer arrived. While there had been other letters, this was the first one received since learning of her birth. It was much shorter than usual. Referring to our daughter's situation, he simply ended it with the words, "Aren't we glad she is ours?"

Does the word "honor" come to mind?

MORE MALAPRYORISMS

It is hard to describe the joy of just listening to Jack talk. Often he says the most profound things and doesn't even realize it.

Many of us have gone through this experience, haven't we? When they were the right age to enjoy them we bought our daughters a play-sized oven and refrigerator for Christmas. Unfortunately, more than a little assembly was required. As the holiday grew closer and closer I asked mechanically challenged Jack to stop delaying and get them put together. He said he didn't have to hurry because all he had to do was take them out of their boxes and read the destructions. You can imagine the rest.

Taking a page out of Yogi Berra's book of mangled English, he described one of the opponents of his beloved Buffalo Bills as unmerciless. When I asked him who wrote a book he was raving about and thought I might like to read he said he didn't know the author because he used a pseudo name. When I corrected him and said that he probably meant to use the word non de plume or pseudonym he said I didn't pronunce my words right.

Once while wondering about a woman who hadn't been seen at church for a while he said she never came near there most of the time anymore. After listening to and advising a man with a troubled family history he said his only regret was that he had been unsuccessful in showing him the terror of his ways.

He likes to store things in gallon size grid-lock plastic bags and sometimes wears a wet suit to protect himself from hydrothermia.

Getting a bit more graphic, I've been told that I don't know which side my butt is breaded on. I'm also not supposed to get my knockers in a knit. And, much to the surprise of the Hebrew nation, in their religious rites, they were to offer lambs, rams, and buttocks.

Who knew?

IMMERSED IN HIS WORK

The long year of separation was finally over. When Jack, now Captain Pryor, returned to the United States, a large group of his family met him at the airport. There for the first time he met his seven month old daughter. We--now three--were finally united.

Soon Jack joined his father in the family business. Quickly, the public side of him emerged. Without even trying he found himself enjoying social clubs, serving in civic groups and even elected to the local School Board. He particularly liked attending a business men's religious group where he met and became friends with a man named, Al. Bonding immediately, these two did all they could to encourage and support each other.

Pastor Al was well known and often got invited to speak and minister at various venues in our area and beyond. When weather permitted he was also asked to officiate at outdoor water baptisms held during retreats at a camp on beautiful Lake George in the Adirondack Mountains.

One particular baptism was especially memorable. Many men had come to the camp that year. Of these, many more men than usual asked to be baptized. Thinking that some assistance would be welcome Al sought out Jack who was also at the retreat and asked him if he would help at the ceremonies. Never one to pass up ministry and have fun at the same time, Jack said yes.

The next day all met at the agreed time. Al explained the meaning of water baptism, asked each man if he understood the doctrine, agreed with it and chose to take part in it. The willing ones were then instructed on how it would happen. One by one each would enter the lake, either cross his arms over his chest or hold his nose, allow Al and Jack to tip him backward into and under the water, and, finally, to allow them to pull him out. When finished each was free to leave or he could stand on shore and cheer on any others eager to honor God.

With these preliminaries over, Al and Jack stepped into the water. They realized immediately that the lake bed was not pebbles or stones; it was mud. This created two problems. The first was quickly overcome when, to keep themselves from sliding in the slippery ooze, they dug their feet in until suction from the mud glued them to the bottom.

The second situation had no solution. The mud had a mind of its own. It was not content to continue to lie on the bottom of the lake. It became quite frisky when dozens of feet tromped on it. Detaching itself from the lake bed it proved that it could spread out like a dingy blanket in the water in just no time at all.

The initial candidates for baptism were the smart ones. They stepped into pristine water and their footsteps and immersions left the lake a bit roiled. The next several men stepped into silty water and their commotion left the water murky. The majority of men had to step into and get dipped into dirty water. Small wonder that afterward many chose to go for a quick dip in another part of the lake to get cleaned off rather than stay and watch the ceremony.

Because of these conditions one man in the last group had an especially memorable baptism. It began innocently enough. Like the others before him, he stepped into the lake, crossed his arms, took a deep breath, got tipped backward and disappeared momentarily under the muddy waters.

Only it wasn't momentarily.

He didn't come back up.

Jack thought Al was holding on to him and Al assumed that Jack was. In truth neither was and the man, hidden by the dirty water, had floated away. While neither dared say anything to the group who were watching on the shore they both knew something had to be done. Fast!

Suddenly Al and Jack began what looked like a curious courting ritual. While Al tried to pull his feet free of the mud Jack bent over, shielded his eyes from the sun and tried to look for the missing man in the turbid water. Then they reversed movements. Al now bent to look and Jack stood to unsuction his feet. Up and down they bobbed. No floating objects were sighted and time was marching on.

Next, both plunged hands and arms underwater and flailed around trying to find the victim. Al tried long, up and down arm sweeps while Jack used circling motions. The lost stayed lost while time was passing.

On they danced. Feet now free, Al kicked out to the right and Jack to the left to probe for the more-than-immersed body. There was no sign of him.

Tension was mounting.

Where was he?

How long had he been under water?

Do you believe in miracles? Al and Jack do. Suddenly, simultaneously, both men felt something bump into their legs. Praying that the lost was found they quickly bent over, reached into the water, grabbed the escapee and pulled him upright.

Anxiously they asked if he was all right.

Sputtering and gasping for breath, he assured them that he was. Then a beautiful smile overspread his face. "I feel very close to God," he said.

How close he will never know.

SKI BUM

Some things start out well and go downhill from there. Just so, they don't call it downhill skiing for nothing.

After Jack returned from overseas he spent the next twenty-five years working in cable TV. This new industry was growing and changing quickly as it strove to move in position from new kid on the block to a viable local, state, national and world wide business. When schedules and meetings and managing got too hectic Jack was wise enough to take time away from it all. On one such occasion, we decided to go to Vermont for a ski vacation.

Jack was a fairly good skier. I was not. Often his version of a delightful run was to whiz down a slope and wait for me at the bottom. My idea of a delightful run was to live through it. I didn't whiz anywhere. Instead, my style of skiing resembled a duck in a shooting gallery. In a deliberate attempt to keep my speed down I would ski to my right for about fifty feet, do a slippery about face and ski another fifty feet to my left eventually zigzagging my way down the hill. I probably covered five times more ground and took five times as long to complete each run as Jack did. As you can imagine this meant that I was always behind him. (Yes, one of several very bad puns.)

One day of our ski getaway was particularly memorable. After deciding to try some new slopes we quickly found ourselves on the backside of nowhere. Unfortunately we also found ourselves half way down a hill that branched out in two directions giving us the dubious choices of Black Diamond runs that (to my terrified mind) should have been labelled "If You Pray, You Might Live Through This" and "Instant Death". Either was beyond my ability to negotiate but side stepping way, way, way back up the hill in the midst of dozens of turbo charged skiers did not seem like a safe option either. We decided to press on.

Checking both trails to see which seemed least dangerous we opted for the one on the right. This canted down at an alarming angle and led all skiers toward a right angle turn that was heavily banked with snow and crowned by an orange fence which warned of a hundred foot drop off should any choose to go over, under, or through it. From there the trail veered sharply to the left and sloped down, down, down until at its bottom we could see ant-like creatures winding their way toward the ski lift.

Knowing I was scared, Jack volunteered to go first. Just as he pushed off for the first leg of his rescue mission I spotted what seemed like a strip of cloth hanging down behind him. Noticing that it was the same dark blue color of his ski pants, I hoped all was well.

Part way down the hill, he stopped to allow me to catch up. As soon as I did so, he again went on ahead of me. This time as he skied away there were two dark strips flying out behind him. I now recognized them as the straps to his bib overalls. Thinking that this could not be good I decided that when I caught up to him again I should tell him that something was amiss.

Sadly that never happened. When I again skied up to him and opened my mouth to warn him, he continued the pattern we had established and was instantly off for the third time. Intent on getting us down the slope he had no time for idle chit chat.

The dangling straps had indeed been a harbinger of dire things to come. Now as he skied away I could see something else. A gap seemed to be opening near his waist. Between his bright red jacket and his navy blue pants I could now see something that was light blue. Realizing that the clips attaching the straps to his bib overalls had both failed, I watched in unbelief as the light blue gap grew wider and wider. Even as he drew further away from me I got a perfect view of a red jacket, dark blue pants that were now bunched up at his knees and an open-to-the air derriere decked out in light blue long johns.

Jack, maybe from the sudden blast of cold air, was now aware that he had a problem. Handicapped by the entangling pants, he couldn't successfully use his feet to slow himself, turn or stop. In a futile attempt to ward off disaster he threw away his ski poles, reached down, grabbed his disappearing pants and tried to pull them up again. No such luck. The frisky trousers were not done with their own downhill run. Eluding his grasp they descended as far as they could and then enthroned themselves on the tops of his boots. Since this effectively removed any hope of maneuvering his skies, Jack crashed. Flipping over on his back and with feet in the air he slid head first down the trail toward and then stopping just shy of the orange fence.

There he lay. His pants were entangling his feet so he could not separate them far enough apart to plant the edges of his skies in the snow and use them for the leverage needed to stand up. His light blue thermal underwear had also succumbed to the law of gravity. They too had begun a long descent and were now wound around his knees.

I managed to ski down to within fifty feet of him. Others streaking down the same slope saw the problem and began to stop, too. Congregating in groups of twos or threes, all we could see was a kaleidoscope of wildly thrashing body parts clad in red, light blue and navy blue-and now white.

Slowly others who were trying to negotiate both the dangerous curve and the body sprawled in the middle of it inched their way over to Jack. Two men managed to get on either side of him, grab an arm, and pull him upright. Still a bit shaken, he just stood there for a minute in his multicolored ensemble. Suddenly realizing where he was and how he looked, he turned his back toward us and bent over to find and hoist his missing pants. It was then that I realized that if the BVD barrier hadn't held all of us watching would really have been exposed to a ski bum.

When at last he had gotten himself together and every layer of clothing was again where it should be, he wisely knotted the two straps to his ski pants around his neck so there would be no repeat adventures. Without even looking at me or the now sizable crowd he took off like a shot, flew down the hill and disappeared. Realizing I was left on the hill to find my own way down I began my own descent. Slowly making turn after turn I finally reached the bottom intact. Even while I was wondering how to find a map to learn where I was or where a member of the Ski patrol might be I heard, "Pssst!"

Looking around I spotted Jack peeking out from the side of an outbuilding. When I skied over to him our tender reunion was short lived. Since he wanted to be out of the area sooner than immediately he started skiing toward the gondola. There his worst fears were confirmed. It began with the pointing and laughing. Then he heard shouts of, "Hey! It's him!" or "I missed it. Could you do it again?" When the clapping started he bolted. Our down hill skis quickly became cross country skis as we flew through woods and fields. When at last we came to a service road we hitched a ride back to our condo with some amenable resort workers.

He said it was to get there more quickly because he was cold.

I knew it was so he wouldn't be the butt of any more jokes.

TILES in TIBERIAS

Have you ever met anyone who was unflappable? I mean someone able to remain calm, cool and collected in any situation? Have you ever wondered how to handle an embarrassing situation? Let Jack, the master, instruct you.

Several years ago after reading about it and hearing others describe its novelty Jack and I decided to take a trip to Israel. Finding a great group to tour with, off we went.

I can't say that we enjoyed the usual sights because nothing in Israel seemed usual. For instance, when we arrived and deplaned we knew we were in for an amazing time when two perfectly arched, fully colored rainbows overspread the sky.

We visited the regions of Jesus' birth, youth, and ministry. Toward the end of the trip on one very meaningful day we were baptized in the Jordan River. Therein lies the tale.

Our trip to the Holy Land took place in November. As we soon learned, that was rainy-going-into-winter season. Some days were desert hot and arid while others were stormy. The day we went to the Jordan was just plain dank, drizzly and very cool. You can well imagine then that arriving at the baptismal spot, changing our clothes, standing in cold rain while awaiting our turn and getting immersed in the frigid, fast flowing water of the Jordan River left us shivering. Even changing back into dry clothes did little to warm us. By the time we arrived at our hotel in Tiberias we were chilled to the bone.

This hotel was new and our group was among the first to enjoy its amenities. Four walls of guest accommodations rose up many stories from an open, central courtyard. Immediately after checking in, we wet ones, giddy at the thought of a long, hot shower, ran for our rooms. In our case Jack won the race. He was stripped and in the shower before I even had my suitcase in the door. When he was warmed and finished he put on his pajamas, popped into bed and was instantly asleep.

Having the facilities all to myself I too delighted in a lengthly, leisurely, hot shower. In spite of the many times I had told our children that five minutes was surely enough time to get all body parts more than clean I ignored my own instructions. I lingered. I dawdled, I reveled in every steamy moment.

Finally finished, I decided not to sleep. Instead I opted to go down to the courtyard for a cup of tea. Just as I left our room and locked the door it happened. A sudden, horrendous, literally earth shaking cacophony of sound exploded around me, thundered up and down the corridor and echoed up and down the multi-tiered open atrium of the hotel.

The reaction was instantaneous. All over our floor doors opened and panicked people began running. Women were screaming in alarm and children were crying. Since we were after all in Israel many assumed that our hotel had been the target of hostile fire.

Exhausted Jack slept through all this. He also slept through the immediate arrival of the hotel security guards who did a preliminary check for damage. Following their every move, those of us in the hall were relieved to discover that they could not find any sign of enemy attack and that the hotel seemed fully intact. They concluded that whatever had caused the deafening crash had come from within, not without.

Relieved but yet concerned, the guests began to disperse. Since all desire for a cup or tea was now gone I returned to our room. I realized, you see, that all was not as it should be. Though its origin had not yet been discovered, I knew that the epicenter of this situation was somewhere very near us.

Jack slept on as I checked our bedroom. All seemed well. He slept on as I opened the door to our bathroom. There I couldn't believe what I was seeing.

Apparently loosened by our long, steamy, watery indulgences, every tile surrounding our new shower had loosened from the walls, slammed down into the bathtub and shattered. Bits, pieces, and shards of ceramic now covered every surface. Their noisy smashing and breaking was the cause of the explosive din that had echoed out from this tiny room and caused the pandemonium in the corridors.

Running outside I found members of our group who I did know and still frightened guests that I did not. I explained what had happened and to calm them down I invited them into our bathroom to see the smashed rubble.

Apparently some of the din was finally heard by the sleeping Jack. Or maybe it was just that nature was calling. Unknown to me, while I was out in the hall he roused from sleep, got up, and went into the bathroom. In his groggy condition he never noticed the thousands of bits of tile that littered every surface or realized that he was standing on fragments of glass.

What happened next gives new meaning to the meteorological term "jet steam heading south." Just as he began to do what he needed to do I and twenty or so of my new best friends streamed into our room. Perhaps six or seven of these crowded with me into our bathroom.

The reflection of our faces in the mirror said it all. I was stunned speechless. Jack was surprised but unable to stop what he had started. The rest of the group just stood in jaw-dropped amazement.

No one moved.

No one spoke.

After the first startled moment a near riot broke out. Even while the group in the bedroom was still trying to push into the bathroom to see the bare walls and shattered tiles, the group in the bathroom began en masse to back pedal out into the bedroom. When everyone except Jack was finally in our sleeping area I managed to say with a straight face that such sight seeing was no longer an option.

Others were not so circumspect. As more learned what had happened giggles became roars of laughter. Now even more people came into the room or gathered in the corridor to see what had changed fear to funny so quickly.

Suddenly the bathroom door opened. Just as suddenly silence descended. Jack stepped into our midst. Knowing there was nothing to do, he simply said, "Shalom."

The Bible records a story about Moses who parted the Red Sea allowing the Hebrew children to walk through walls of water to safety and security. Here, the crowd parted and Jack walked through walls of people back to the safety and warmth of his bed where he again fell asleep. Even as Moses had diffused the first situation successfully by his actions so now Jack diffused this less important moment by his own calm actions.

Who could have handled it better?

Later down in the courtyard I had something a lot stronger than tea to drink.

BOB

Some of Jack's verbal blunders are just too good to be one liners. Instead of being hurried through they should be savored in a setting all their own. More of them will appear as separate stories.

For instance Bob, my cousin's husband, was outgoing, personable, and thoroughly honest. As a man of character, his wife never lacked love, honor, or protection. Unlike those whose heavy handed discipline led to fear, rebellion, and wrong relationships with their children, as a fun-to-be-with father his light touch led to love, obedience, and right relationships. As a business man trained in economics and monetary resources, his coworkers and the clients who trusted him with their financial futures never doubted his intent or integrity. We, his extended family, loved him as a man who knew himself, was comfortable with himself and who exuded his own particular brand of enthusiasm and joy every day in every way.

Death claimed him way too soon.

When all the red tape and legal entanglements had been resolved Bob came home to New York State. In shock and sorrow his funeral arrangements began in earnest. Surely we've all heard of wedding planners but, much to our surprise, upon accompanying our cousin to the church where his service would be held, we were assigned a funeral planner.

If we were still living in the Dark Ages, this one would have been an ideal choice. In today's world however, she was a bit out of touch.

Obviously skilled in towing the company line rather than in being an angel of mercy and compassion in this time of suffering and loss, she would not accede to even one family wish regarding choices of scripture, readings, or music. Her dour attitude never allowed her to imagine that we could or would desire that Bob's memorial be a gathering to celebrate his life rather than to mourn his death.

In the midst of this Jack and I were asked to speak at the upcoming service. Wholly apart from the rites and rituals of the funeral mass, we were requested to present a light hearted remembrance of Bob, the man. Determined that our contribution to his memory would not include more sorrow, trauma and tears we knew we were about to run afoul of the FP.

We plotted our course, We elicited fond memories from his family. Friends and coworkers contributed their amusing stories. Finally we added our own thoughts of good times spent together. Then, in strict secrecy we compiled, edited and rearranged them all into what we hoped would be a mood lifting ten minute presentation that would leave those gathered with a smile and a twinkle rather than a tear in their eyes.

The day for the funeral dawned. Unusual for mid-July in western New York, even in the very early morning hours of this summer day it was already damp and steamy. By ten o'clock, the air was thick, clothes were damp and hair was curly. Everything we touched was sticky.

And it was at ten o'clock that Jack and I got together to speak. We related a few amusing stories and then it was Jack's privilege to describe Bob's character starting with his humbleness. Unconsciously though he managed to mix up the weather with the event and ran into a little difficulty in his delivery.

In those oppressive weather conditions where he was sweating profusely he whipped out his very large, white handkerchief, wiped his perspiring brow, and in the sultry heat began to speak.

"Bob was a very humid man," he said, "and in his humidity....."

Fortunately the funeral was at eleven o'clock and this was just a practice run. Just as fortunately the FP was not there to hear or she would not have been very humid in her comments to us.

LET'S FACE IT

Countenance---*the face or features, expression or appearance*

Incontinence---*exercising no control over the appetites; sexual passion; unrestrained or, medically speaking, the inability to control your bladder or hold back bodily discharges*

As you can see, there is a big difference between the two words. A big, big difference!

After we bought our first home, we met a lovely ninety year old woman who lived a couple of doors down the street. She was a feisty and forthright neighbor. She honored the memory of her husband from the moment of his death until that of her own. Among other things, she loved her God and was an earnest prayer warrior on behalf of any who loved Him, too.

Over the years we enjoyed her company. Sadly over time, we could see that she had begun to decline. During one difficult Thanksgiving season she struggled with some health issues. Our daughters and I visited her on several occasions to see if we could help or to ask if there was anything she needed. Thankfully, each time we saw her, we could see that she was slowly recovering.

That is, until we dropped in on her at Christmas time. That particular day Jack, who had missed some of the intervening visits, went with us. After hearing our positive reports on how well she was recuperating, I am sure he meant to compliment her on how refreshed she looked. However, speaking in his own special way, when he opened the door and saw her he said, "Why, Mrs. B., your incontinence is so much better."

That set her back just a bit.

FILL 'ER UP!!

Several years ago, as happens to many males, Jack had pushed, pulled, lifted, tennised, worked out, and carried too many heavy objects. As a result, he had developed a hernia.

At first, it was easy to ignore. As time wore on though, occasional discomfort became nagging pain. Nagging pain became chronic pain. Chronic pain became too difficult to deal with every day. Finally a doctor was consulted and a time was set in his schedule for surgery.

The big day came and all went well. With everything nicely tucked back into its rightful place, Jack was moved to a recovery room. There, after he had rested he was told that there was a container in the bathroom and as soon as he had deposited a collectible urine specimen in it, he could be released to go home. I think the actual words of the nurse were, "When we know your insides are working again, we can get you out of here."

So far, though nerve racking, this out patient procedure had been a non-event. Oh, how soon that was to change.

A couple of hours later when Jack was rested, alert, and eager to cooperate with the container, the door opened and into the room came a gurney with another gentleman on it who had just had the same surgery. In a general way, he looked quite like Jack so extra identification bands were put on both of them and their clothing and medical charts were separated. The recent arrival, in his groggy state, was also told about the container awaiting him and what he was supposed to do with it. Then came the already familiar refrain, "When we know your insides are working, we can get you out of here."

When the gurney was removed and his roommate was comfortably placed in bed, Jack made his way to the bathroom and did his thing. His insides were indeed working. Proudly he came back to his bed and sat down to await the moment he was told he was released. While we were planning how to get him to the car and whether we would drive him directly home or stop at the pharmacy on the way, we heard the other gentleman get out of his bed and proceeded to the other room. Since, in his grogginess he had not closed the door and since hospitals are not known to place privacy issues on the top of their to-do lists, it was very quickly obvious to us that he, too, had succeeded in making his contribution. He too came back to his bed, rang the bed bell, and awaited the arrival of the nurse.

Soon she breezed into the room. Addressing Jack first, she asked it he had been successful. "Oh, yes," he said. "My donation is in the container in the bathroom."

Asking the other man the same question, she received his assurance that he too had given his all and the results were ready for her inspection.

She went into the bathroom. There was a long pause. Chatty Cathy was quite quiet. Too quiet.

When she came back into the main room she was flustered. "All right now," she said. "Which of you really left the sample?"

Two hands went up.

Now perturbed, she continued the inquisition. "Then why is there only one container with urine in it?" she questioned.

There was one of those awful moments. It couldn't be. Could it be? Had both men filled the same container?

Now the nurse began intense questioning. Under oath to tell the whole truth, Jack recalled going into the bathroom, filling his container to about half full and leaving it on the shelf above the sink just as he had been told to. Mr. Groggy sort of remembered sleepwalking to the bathroom, seeing a container that was half full, deciding that must be the official one, and proceeded to fill it up. There were two men and one sample. In spite of ample evidence that their "insides were working," both were told to go back to bed.

You can imagine the rest. Just as you can't make a watched pot boil, you can't produce a urine sample from an empty bladder on demand. Both men sat there with a how-did-this-happen expression in their eyes and the look of grim determination in their jaws. Minutes went by. An hour passed. The required specimen did not.

Since by now I had been waiting a long time, I was tempted to offer to donate to the cause in Jack's name but finally, finally, the long wait was over. Jack gave his all in the new container with his name on it that he had been provided with and he was released to go home.

On the ride home I asked what had taken so long in the bathroom. He sheepishly said, " You really don't know how hard it was just to fill my own jar and stop. I really wanted to fill mine and then leave a donation in his to give him something to remember me by."

WILD ONE

Over the years people have commented on Jack's resemblance to Steve Martin. It isn't so much in looks though both are quite handsome. It is more mannerisms, gestures, and zany way of life.

While recuperating from the hernia surgery, Jack decided to spend some of the required down time teaching one of our children how to play Hawaiian Rummy. An old family favorite, the point of this game was to acquire runs and sets in increasing degrees of difficulty. The rules were a bit complicated for a beginner to grasp so he repeated them. As a final instruction, he said, "And don't forget that douches are wild."

I didn't disagree with him.

I just wanted to know how he knew that.

OH, DEER!

It is said that animals are very good at understanding weather patterns. They are said to be harbingers of bad weather and upcoming storms. We should have known then that the adorable deer who was eating at a bird feeder outside our kitchen window that Christmas Eve was trying to tell us something. The next morning, Christmas Day, we woke up to thirty-three inches of snow whose water content was so heavy that when the sun came out it was a gorgeous light blue. We didn't get plowed out for two weeks.

What did all that have to do with Jack? None of us knew that feeding a deer would open the door to all kinds of problems. It was the opening round of what we refer to Deer Wars at our house.

Read on.

The next year, Rudolph returned. He was not alone though. Instead, he brought a friend and the two, wanting more than just bird feed, included myrtle and rhododendrons on their menu.

By 1983 we realized that his friend must have been a girl because we now had Rudolph, his friend and three babies peering up at us. Baby deer don't shoo; they just chew. Our garden was now being systematically stripped of euonymus in the winter and tulips and day lilies in the summer. Dangling aluminum pie pans from fences to flash in the breeze did nothing to discourage their visits.

By 1987 there were ten deer in assorted family groups. Now Jack determined this was his own private war. He alone would be in charge of deer management. He tried leaving clumps of human hair out to prevent the night raids. The deer just laughed. Jack did not.

When 1993 arrived, so did fifteen deer. Jack set out mothballs. The deer snickered. He put up a six foot fence. They easily jumped over it. He put up an eight foot fence. They bounded over it with room to spare. To add to his chagrin, they even went under it and finally through it to get to their food. His only comment was that if they had a family tree, they would probably eat that, too.

Around the year 2000, there was another incident that made all the others pale in comparison. Somehow Rudolph, Dasher, Dancer, and all the rest of the Christmas crew plus assorted female friends and several generations of children and grandchildren again breached all barriers and found their way to my flowers and bird feeders. Jack saw red. Adding up the mounting costs or replacing plants every spring, he fumed.

He decided it was time for the latest weapon in his no-does campaign. Remembering that he had ordered a product through the mail that was guaranteed to repel deer and determined to win this battle with the interlopers, he marched out to the garage to look for it. There he found a large bottle of liquid whose smell was just plain gross. Finding several old tee shirts, he tore them into pieces and dipped them into the stuff. He then spent the rest of the afternoon tying them to a rope and attaching the rope to the bloodied and bowed deer fence. Smugly he knew that he had won. When the deer got one whiff of that awful smell they would go elsewhere for their dining pleasure.

The only problem was that Jack had been standing downwind when he did all of this and the liquid had been blowing and spraying on him all afternoon. The mystery fluid had now saturated his clothing.

While he was outside this had not been too noticeable. When he came in the house that all changed. I made some remarks that he thought were very ungracious about the aroma that was emanating from him. When I mentioned that he might want to strip, set his clothes outside for burning and take a shower he was taken aback. He had been expecting high praise for his determined efforts out in the cold and snow to save our home from marauders and all he got were comments about how he smelled. In a huff, he grabbed a cup of coffee and a newspaper and stalked off to the den. There he enthroned himself on our sofa and sat in sulky silence.

When the odor followed him, I got curious. What could possibly be causing such a nauseating, foul stench? Going out to the garage I found the bottle of deer repellent. Could it really be? It seemed that Jack had been dousing himself in coyote urine. Worse, it wasn't just ordinary coyote urine; it was concentrated coyote urine. Instead of this product out in the garden repelling deer we had concentrated coyote urine in the house gagging us.

Finally even Jack, all but embalmed by the overpowering stench, agreed that there was a problem. Sad to say, the coyote urine that was on his clothing had spread onto the couch as well. Infiltrating the fabric, its saturated back and cushions were unfurling their own obnoxious odors. The temperature was about fifteen degrees out when we began opening every door and window.

That might have seemed like a good idea but it was not. Our cats had gotten in on the act. One by one they filed into the den. They took umbrage. They sniffed him. They circled. They held their noses. While we were busy elsewhere airing out the house they got up on the couch where Jack had been sitting and sniffed some more. Apparently thinking some outraged coyote was threatening their cushy life style, they did what cats do best. Challenging the awful odor, they sprayed their own delightful aromas on to the cushions and down all the inner parts. So prolific were they in their donations that cat drippings now joined coyote urine and both dribbled and oozed their way down the back of the cushions and into the bowels of the couch.

Was Jack upset? No. In fact, he told us to do nothing because it would all dry up and be OK. The next day, the smell was worse. It had dried up but it was not OK. The day after that was even more ghastly and we ordered gas masks. The following day the smell was overpowering and we ordered a new couch.

This was not victory over the deer; it was a complete rout.

To this day, when you visit us, if you should see a deer or smell an unusual odor it probably would be a good idea not to mention it.

THE TEETOTALER

When summer rolls around, we always plan a family party on the Fourth of July. As happens in so many other homes around the nation on that day, we, as hosts, call our kin and graciously---thankfully---make plans with them as they ask what they can bring to the event. That leaves us to provide the main course and beverages.

A couple of days before one recent 4th, I asked Jack what I should plan for drinks. After we figured out who might want what, I asked him specifically what his preferences were. His answer: "I don't want any thing except pop this year."

Surprised by that, I asked him why not.

"I don't want to drink any wine or beer this year," he loftily informed me, "because I have taken a vow of obstinance."

HIS JUST DESSERTS

Jack has traveled enough in his life to know that good food exists outside the kitchen of his home... an understatement if ever there was one. Trips to Europe, Asia, and South America have definitely left an impression on his palette. There are days when his chief delight is to drag anyone willing enough to go with him off to a restaurant where foreign food is being served and enjoy a good meal with good company.

Among others, we have wined and dined with the French, Mexicans, Chinese, Portuguese and Dutch and learned that each had a wonderful, different spice of life. Unfortunately, Jack's command of the English language does not necessarily match his acumen with a menu. You can imagine therefore that there have been some memorable as well as delicious moments at table with him.

One particular evening we were exploring the delights of Greek cuisine. After a delightful meal of Greek salad and moussaka, the waiter asked if we would like dessert. Eyes lighting up at the very thought of it, Jack quickly spoke up and said, "I would like a bossa nova."

Completely at a loss, the waiter explained that the restaurant did not serve that for dessert and asked if he would like to see a menu to make a selection among those things that were available. Realizing that he had made a mistake, he recovered himself nicely, refused the menu and said, " I've changed my mind. I'll have some balaclava."

He sat in sulky silence while the rest of us enjoyed some particularly delicious baklava and he was served coffee with a mint.

THE I'S HAVE IT

This last summer, Jack's wrist began to bother him. Afraid that it might be a problem with carpel tunnel and remembering the difficulties his sister had when she had been diagnosed with that, he finally went to see a doctor.

When called into the office, he held up his right arm, ran his fingers along the top of it near his wrist and expressed his anxiety about the soreness. After a bit of probing and some twisting and turning of his wrist, the doctor said that no, he didn't think Jack had a carpel tunnel problem. Rather, he thought it was an inflamed tendon. His prescription:
1. Get a wrist brace and wear it as often as he could
2. Get a six week supply of ibuprofen and take it faithfully as prescribed
3. At the end of the six weeks come in for a reevaluation.

Army-quick to follow an order, after leaving the doctor's office, Jack drove directly to the pharmacy. There he bought the wrist brace.

And, there he bought six weeks worth of -------Immodium.

When he got home and innocently announced this,

my immediate reactions surprised him. Not really sure if he was just joking, I first asked to see the "prescription." Sure enough, there nestled in its own little bag was a mountain of boxes of Immodium. To save his feelings, I tried desperately hard to contain myself. Failing that, I burst into uncontrollable laughter. Speechlessly he watched until I reached the point that tears were running down my face and I had to sit down, wrap my arms around my midsection and just hold myself together.

When I could finally speak again he asked me what was so funny. I explained to him what both OTC drugs were and what each was supposed to be used for. My final comment was, "After six weeks of Immodium, you won't have to worry about your wrist anymore. You are going to be a lot sorer and tenderer somewhere else."

His final comment was, "At least they both started with an I."

PRESERVING THE POINSETTIAS

Christmas has always been a special time at our house. Not only is it the celebration of the birth of the Savior of the world but also it is the holiday in which beautiful decorations suddenly adorn everything in sight. At our house, we don't stop at just decking the halls with boughs of holly. We fill every space or cover every place with trees, ornaments, angels, bells, balls, and all sorts of cheery, festive things.

One big feature or our holiday décor is plants. We never feel we are fully decorated until the smell of boxwood permeates the air or the sight of appropriately placed pine roping, wreaths, and greenery delight the eye. Further, as the years have passed, we have steadily increased the number of poinsettias that we add to the floral mix so that each plant, ensconced in its place, seems to be a bright spot of beauty to those of us who have to endure the blahs of a colorless western New York winter.

Last year, something very special happened concerning our plants that will long be remembered when we gather as family to laugh over past events.

After we had decorated the tree and arranged the greens, it was time to go on the annual poinsettia hunt.

Bundling into the car on a night when the wind was howling and the snow was falling, Jack and I went to the store. Even as we walked in, we found banks of the colorful live beauties ready for our inspection. White, cream, pink, and red plants were just preening before us trying to catch our eye so they would end up in our cart and eventually in our home.

These were nice but they were not perfect. Jack patiently waited while I carefully looked at each one. Finally, I decided they just didn't pass the test and we would have to find the special ones we were looking for somewhere else.

Just then, an employee who had noticed my meticulous examination walked over and inquired, "Have you seen the poinsettias in the garden shop?"

Not really wanting to face the raw weather again and knowing it had already been a long day for one of us who had spent hours on a ladder festooning everything he could reach with things handed up to him from others of us wise enough to keep our feet firmly planted on the floor, I decided to check them out before trying another store.

Off we trotted to the garden section. One step inside the door and it was like being in the middle of a rainbow. As lovely as the other arrangement of plants had been, these were beyond merely lovely. These were gorgeous.

Beauty was everywhere. Every color that poinsettias came in was represented there. Every size they came in was found there. They were strong, vibrant, and glorious. No need for inspection. These were it! Best of all, though it was yet weeks before Christmas, they were on sale for half price.

We loaded up one cart with plants and carried the rest. Proudly we protected the little beauties through the checkout line and then escorted them home. We placed them in living and dining rooms, den, hall, powder room, kitchen and even office. Everywhere that they rested in state they perked up spirits and brought a special beauty. Each was a spot of glory existing to honor the birth of the Babe.

My husband was so taken by my joy in their brightness and my delight in their radiance that, as a special gift of love, he decided to appoint himself a one-man team of caretakers. That evening I found him rummaging in our garage until he found an old grow-light, an artificial source of light that gardeners use to force seeds to sprout or to keep plants healthy.

Next, as a test run, he gathered all the poinsettias and placed them on our kitchen table. Then, he pounded a nail in a cabinet, strung up the grow-light, and plugged it in. Obviously pleased with the attention and care, the poinsettias seemed to radiantly offer their thanks.

In the morning, he reversed the process. He took down the lamp, gathered the flowers and replaced them in their designated spots of display.

Christmas season is deliberately prolonged at our house. We enjoy it from the day after Thanksgiving when we revel in "decorate-the-house-day" until New Year's Day when we sadly take all the decorations down. Since, during some years, this can last as long as six weeks, you can therefore imagine the herculean effort, the persistence, and the determination in Jack's elongated effort to preserve the beauty of the Christmas plants.

Following his established pattern, I watched in amazement when, every night, he would gather up the flowers, trundle them to the kitchen, place them just so on the table and light them up. He was such a good plant steward that he even rotated the crop. At times, the white and light ones would be in the middle of the bunch on the table and the pinks and reds would be relegated to the outside edges of the massed plants. Then another night he would reverse it and the pinks and reds occupied center stage and the paler ones were on the fringes. The small ones always got preferential seating so the tall ones could not overshadow them and block out the light.

I watched in awe as every morning he returned them to their designated spot and arranged them so their beauty was most obvious.

Several times a week in the midst of all this effort my budding florist would say, "Look! Aren't they beautiful?" or "They're just thriving! The reds are still very colorful and we haven't lost a single leaf yet."

Smiling secretly, I could only agree with him. The plants were indeed every bit as beautiful as the day we had brought them home from the store.

All too soon came the day we all dreaded. Take down day. Even though he knew he was nearing the end of his duties as flower farmer, Jack still bathed his beauties in light the night before they were to disappear and again exclaimed on the richness of their color and the health of their stems and leaves. So fond had he become of his buds and blossoms that he almost cried when, after all the decorations were taken down, stowed in their appropriate boxes, and stored under the eaves in the attic it was time to take the poinsettias, even in their still pristine glory, out to the garage.

That night, bereft of the flowers he had so diligently cared for, he slowly dismantled his grow-light that he thought had done such a wonderful job of keeping the plants vibrant for the whole of the Christmas season and sadly put it away.

It was probably a full week later that I worked up the courage to tell him that although the first grouping of poinsettias we had looked at were alive, the ones we had bought were not. They had been displayed in a different area and were available at such a good price because they were in truth only imitation.

What then was the point of letting him go on for weeks laboring under the illusion that he was preserving my poinsettias? It was to savor the fullness of his real gift. You see, caring for flowers was not his present to me last Christmas; seen in its right light, that was simply the outer working or manifestation of his real gift. The presents from his heart, the expressions of his time and love to serve me in such a way that was so special to me, were his true Christmas gifts, ones that I will now take the time to gather, shine the light on, and make every effort to cherish and preserve for as long as I live.

JUST PUTTERING AROUND

Every spring the snow birds, residents of northern states who spend part of the cold months in the south, migrate home. Just so, every spring when the last vestiges of snow are melted away, professional golfers who practice and play in the southern states during winter months, come to our milder climes for some northern exposure.

For many years, Corning, a lovely, small city in New York's Southern Tier, hosted an LPGA event. Since this venue was close to our home, attending became a yearly ritual. When the signs and ads for the upcoming tournament would begin to appear, we would begin to set dates and make arrangements to go. Always there were exciting moments and always a personal memory or two to take away with us. One year stands out above the rest.

Having survived one more long, dark, cold western New York winter, one very pleasant May day beckoned us to drop the agendas, defy the priority list, and burst the chains of duty. All too willing to enjoy a day beaming with sunshine and twittering with bird calls, we popped in the car and drove to the Corning Golf Club.

There, we parked, walked, got our program and decided where to go to sit and watch a morning of really top notch golf. Two ladies in particular were challenging each other for the lead that day and the excitement was mounting for if they maintained the caliber of golf that we were witnessing, surely one of these two would be the tournament winner.

After our lunch break we decided to spend the afternoon following these two. We would join the crowd of fans watching the first and then finish our day enjoying the second.

Accordingly, we staked out our positions and eagerly awaited the duel.

Back and forth it went. First one was ahead and then the other. Finally, a chance came for Judy (not her real name) to go up one. She had hit a great ball off the tee, followed that with an amazing approach shot and now needed but to putt out to birdie the hole.

As she approached the ball, the crowd got silent, No one moved. No one sneezed. We held our collective breaths because we knew how important this stroke would be.

She hit the sure shot----and missed.

The crowd groaned. She moaned. Her face went from eager to unbelieving to just plain mad. After all that work, the score was back to even.

After tapping in with her next attempt, she picked up her ball, stared at it contemptuously and flipped it at her caddy. She then grabbed her offending putter by its head and, without saying a word, stalked off. The next tee was up a long hill. So began the climb muttering to herself while slashing the golf club from right to left and left to right in front of her.

Half way up the hill was an outhouse. For the more genteel, these are also known as Port-a-potties or Port-a johns. This one, standing out clearly in its lonely isolation, sat precariously perched on the steep hillside. Its back end was planted in the ground but it front end was resting on what appeared to be a tipsy, unstable beam.

Sometime during the excitement of the birdie disaster, mother nature had called and Jack had climbed the hill to use the facilities. He was therefore in the outhouse when angry Judy, leading her disheartened fans, charged up the hill. Still her putter slashed. Right. Left. Right. Left. It flew through the air with cuts and slices of ever greater ferocity.

Spying the little house on the hill, a new means of venting her outrage presented itself. As she neared it, she thrust her club to her left and let loose with a mighty swing to the right, striking the port-a potty. The noise of the shot heard around Corning caromed off the hills and echoed through the valleys. Then another whack. And a third--each one so powerful that they threatened to knock the little house off its perch.

Suddenly from deep within the bowels of the outhouse was heard, "Hey, what was that?"

Even with club raised for another shot, Judy, in flabbergasted amazement, stopped her assault. Her face that was already red from anger now turned crimson in embarrassment. After a moment of complete silence the crowd who had been quietly commiserating with Judy burst into laughter.

The voice from within again asked, "What is going on out there?"

Not knowing what else to do, Judy handed her putter to her caddie and continued her uphill climb. As word of what had happened passed from front to back of the crowd, more groups of fans roared with laughter and delight as they too continued to struggle up the slope.

Finally, there was just one older gentleman left. And finally Jack cautiously opened the door of the port-a john. He looked out, stepped out, and again asked what had happened.

"Son," the man said smiling as he walked over and put his arm around Jack's shoulders, "son, I think she just made her first hole in one."

GOLF---2008

You might think that that harrowing experience would sour Jack on golf for life. Think again. It wasn't too much later that Jack decided that he wanted to do more than just go to a golf course and watch others play. He wanted to learn the game. Accordingly, he and a friend spent a summer taking lessons and then, as an immediate follow up, he reinforced them by putting his clubs away and not playing for a year.

Finally the moment came---that particular moment when fear of embarrassing yourself and looking like a fool is overcome by the desire to just try it. When a foursome of equal expertise banded together and agreed to spend a lot of money (gas was then $4.15 a gallon) finding courses that were far, far away, the golf season of 2008 was launched.

Some highlights: Early in the summer, the Fore Putzes found themselves on a rolling course with lovely views and gorgeous sunsets in Naples, New York. On one hole, to the golfer's left a series of two by tens held up by railroad ties were stacked up parallel to the ground to form a fence to keep a small hill from eroding. To avoid this wall of wood, the trick was to hit the ball to the right. When it was Jack's turn to play, he selected his club, stepped up to the tee and swung at his ball, launching it with a hard hit. He then watched in amazement as the ball, with a mind of its own, refused to go to the right. Instead, it chose to fly to the left. In a split second, it smashed into the wooden barrier, did a complete about face and flew backward.

Jack later described this as his whack, crack, and ooopphhh shot. The whack, as you might guess, was the sound of him hitting the ball. The crack was the noise the ball made when it crashed into the wood. And the ooopphhh was the involuntary reaction of another member of the foursome who was hit by the flying ball.

In another moment of glory, Jack was in a bit of difficulty in a sand trap so he was forced to hit a wedge shot. He hunkered down, got his feet in the right position, shortened his swing and let fly. He hit the ball and then, amazingly, the ball hit him. In the knee. Physically impossible? Yes! But, it happened.

Another day, while aiming his ball straight down a fairway, he took the scraggly, bare, dead top branch off a tall tree fifty feet to his left. Foliage abuse or just blind luck?

In a small course in Dansville, New York, (home of Clara Barton of Red Cross fame) a major reconstruction and building project was underway. All golfers were warned, if they chose to play there anyway, to avoid the heavy machinery, construction vehicles, and unusual traffic in and around the various holes.

Paying no attention to that fair warning, Jack, on one hole, stepped up to the tee and drove his ball. Instead of flying true, it veered to the left (are we detecting a southpaw trend here?). It then flew over a small hill and disappeared. When he and his trusty companions climbed the hill and trudged to the area the ball should have been, there were several backhoes and Bobcats in sight but no ball. After searching, even while dodging among the still working machinery, his ball was finally found. It was imbedded in the ground and had tread marks from a caterpillar gloriously decorating it.

Discussion followed and it was decided not to use the mashie on that which was already mashed. It cost him a stroke.

By September of this first-ever year of golf, Jack had become known as Dr. Divot. It was almost a regular sight for him to hit a mighty shot from tee or green and then see the clump of dirt he dug up propel itself through the air for very long distances.

This presented a huge difficulty for the Fore Putzes. To play, they usually divided up into two man teams. After both players from both teams hit their shots, they would then find all four balls, decide which two were the best team shots and, using these two, play on from there. The dilemma then was whether Jack's divots which sometimes went as far as the balls and often landed in a better lie could legitimately be counted as the best shot or not.

And my personal favorite--

A course in Nunda, New York, had fairways that ran parallel to each other with the tee off area of one near the putting green of the another.

One famous day Jack forgot to yell "Fore!" to let other golfers in the area know that there was a ball in the air near them. Again... his ball did not fly exactly where he meant it to go. He watched as it sailed and sailed and landed perfectly on the green. The only problem was that it was not his green; it was the green parallel to him.

No problem. He threw down his club, ran after the ball, watched it bounce once or twice and then roll and roll on the foreign fairway. Finally out of ooomph, it came to a stop between the feet of a gentleman who, club raised and head down for his own next shot, suddenly found himself looking down at two golf balls.

It was just then that an out of breath Jack jogged up, sized up the situation with a single glance, yelled a belated "Fore!", retrieved his ball and jogged away again leaving the other golfer wondering if a trip to the 19th hole was in order.

We can only look forward to next year.

FALLING OUT

Sometimes having a falling out means that a relationship has become strained. Perhaps friends who once enjoyed each other's company are no longer in touch or relatives who once loved each other are estranged. Other times a falling out is a physical act; someone literally falls out of something. It is only the very skillful who manage to combine both versions in one incident. Our story again involves Jack and a sailboat.

Long after the glory days of snipe racing at Loon Lake had passed sailing remained one of Jack's greatest delights. Over the years various boats had come and gone and each was fully enjoyed until its sails were furled for the last time. His present boat is a Phantom. Once quite dashing with its gleaming white deck and orange, yellow and white sail, it is now so old that repair parts can't be found and new sails can't be bought. In other words it is comfortably broken in and sails like a dream.

Unless I am in the boat. Then things get a bit dicey.

Just as Jack never lost his love for sailing over the years, so also he never lost his skill at it. On the other hand, while I too learned to love sailing I never found my skill at it.

Gently realizing that, when we were sailing together, Jack usually did all that needed doing. With the rope of the sail secured in one hand and the tiller in the other who knows how many days we spent sailing into the sun? Or trying to catch the wind just right and sail all the way around the tiny island that graced our lake? Or sneaking up on the sea gulls, geese or migrating loons that were nodding off in our quiet waters? Talk about heaven on earth.

There were however those rare and heady moments when Jack would somewhat reluctantly allow me to "help" sail the boat. Though he wisely never allowed me access to the tiller he would upon occasion let me hold the rope and tend the sail. Inevitably before he did so he would put on his teacher's hat and give me the same two instructions:

I was to wrap the rope around my hand and never, but never, let go of it. Never!

I was to watch the sail and if I saw a fluff in the luff-- whatever that was--I was to pull the rope toward myself until the fluff disappeared.

These instructions usually worked wonderfully well until.........

Several summers ago, Jack and I awoke to the perfect summer day. Bright sunshine cheered us, breezes called us and beauty surrounded us. It was a day made for sailing.

As soon as we had done all we needed to do and were free to do what we wanted to do, we made a dash for the Phantom. The boat impatiently tugged at the buoy while we got ready to sail. In record time we were off.

With Jack on his side of the craft and me on mine we sailed, we tacked, and we came about. Leaning back, thrilling to each wet splash, I was thoroughly enjoying the ride. Then, joy of joys, Jack handed me the rope. Even as he did so I again heard, "...don't ....the rope; .... luff...pull, yadda, yadda, yadda. On we sailed.

A whole afternoon seemed to pass in the blink of an eye. Just as we were thinking of turning back toward home, a breeze sprang up. Catching us all but asleep in the dozy sunshine and fresh air when it hit, Jack flopped over backward and fell out of the boat. I did not. Left alone in the boat the only thing I could do was to clutch my rope for dear life and hang on. There I was in a sail boat without a sailor. That was the first falling out.

Then to my horror, I realized the worst. The boat was still moving. Even as I looked at Jack I knew the distance between us was widening.

Was I nervous? No.

Was I concerned? No way.

Terrorized is more like it. When it became crystal clear that all of Jack's sailing lessons had taught me what to do to make the boat go faster but none of them told me how to make it slow down I panicked.

"What do I do now?" I thought.

"How do I stop?" I shouted.

Over the sound of the breeze he shouted his answer. Sadly, all I could hear was something that sounded like, "How do I cope?" I thought that was what I was asking him.

Maybe though he had yelled, "Here's the dope." That was more like it but he never followed that up with any instructions.

Even while I was straining to listen and then restraining what I thought I had heard to learn how to stop a runaway boat I looked back at Jack. His head was now but a dark dot on the water. I then made the mistake of looking ahead. The shore of the lake was quickly growing larger. If something didn't happen soon I would be crashing into it.

Now my brain went into overdrive. What indeed had Jack yelled to me? Perhaps it was, "I can only hope." Me too. But that didn't stop the boat.

On we sailed, this boat and I, heading for disaster. Things were so perilous that I was now sure his final words were, "Call the Pope." That was good idea if I had my cell phone with me. I didn't know if His Eminence could sail but I had to assume that he could pray.

Other than the mercy of God there is no explanation for what happened next. Just as the boat--with no fluffs in its sail--was choosing between a dock, a moored motor boat or a rocky beach for our head-on crash, a shore wind popped up. Without even waiting to ask if I knew how to come about, it simply swung the front of the boat around and blew us, boat and rider, back out on the lake. Instead of heading away from Jack, I was now on a direct path toward him.

Unbelievably... I watched. Things like this just didn't happen. Yet, if all went well and the boat didn't change course I would be sailing right back to Jack. And just like the old cowboy movies that I once loved to watch where a horse galloped close to John Wayne who could grab the pommel, do a flip and a jump, and find himself in the saddle of the moving animal, so sailor Jack could grab the side, do a belly whump and find his way back aboard our moving boat.

Would you believe that is exactly how it happened? As if choreographed from above, the boat drew close, Jack swam to it and climbed in. Our tender reunion lasted about a minute. Forgetting that divine intervention had saved us, panic now turned into anger. At the very time I said, "Why didn't you tell me what to do?" he said, "Why didn't you do what I told you to do?" Our words clashed in midair.

"What?"I now shouted incredulously. "And just what did you tell me to do?"

Looking down at my hand he quietly said, "I told you to let go of the rope!"

When I too looked I couldn't believe it. To my utter astonishment I was still clutching the rope to the sail. Through the runaway ride, the almost crash and the unearthly rescue I had instinctively done as I had been instructed to do. In obeying his command I thought I had nobly fulfilled my mission. He thought I was nuts. We had just had our second falling out.

Before anything else happened Jack reached over, took the rope and dropped it into the well of the boat. For a while he glared and I had a snit. After we had both fully expressed ourselves and the dust had settled, he indicated that it might be time for another sailing lesson. Apparently those told to hold on to a rope should have the common sense to do so only if they really intended to sail. If they didn't or they wanted to stop sailing, they should know to release the rope. In other words, to his engineering mind, this all boiled down to an equation. A hand holding the rope meant wind in the sail and actual sailing; hands releasing the rope meant no wind in the sail and no sailing, no almost crashing and no need of high seas rescues. Funny time to be telling me that.

Later when we reached home and had eaten peace descended. On the porch watching a spectacular sunset I began to think. In our more public life I of the two of us was the teacher. In the past I loved to lose myself in books, do research, compile notes and make an orderly presentation of them to various groups eager to hear. But in our more private married life, it is Jack who always instructs me. Without the reference books and notes, without even knowing that he is doing so he has taught me things that addressed the issue at hand and then expanded from there to become a new life lesson.

So it was with this. In the quiet of the evening I realized that the words meant to resolve a specific event in our lives had far greater application. In fact they were the answer to some personal problems that had been weighing me down. For instance, if I wanted to change a course of action, why not wait for the right wind and let it turn things around? Or... when I wanted to avoid gossip, why not let the wind out of the conversational sails by just walking away? Or... if I wanted to be rid of negative thoughts, why not let them lie dead in the water? Or... if I needed to opt out of a destructive relationship why not just let go of the rope?

While there is a time to hold on and pull things toward myself there is also a time to let go.

In addition, I realized that a falling out often leads to a falling in. If allowed to, it can result in a better understanding of other people and a deeper relationship with them.

So it was that, after both of our falling outs, I could only thank my Sailor who always had his sails in order, my Teacher who showed me the most remarkable things in the nicest ways, my Engineer who coped with the difficulties of life with workable formulas and my very patient husband for a lovely day.

And I could only thank God that in small measure I do know Jack.

www.ingramcontent.com/pod-product-compliance
Lightning Source LLC
Chambersburg PA
CBHW020917090426
42736CB00008B/668